FROM HEAVEN TO HELL TO HEALED

How to survive and thrive after
a narcissistic, sociopathic relationship

by Dani Leigh

The contents of this work, including, but not limited to, the accuracy of events, people, and places depicted; opinions expressed; permission to use previously published materials included; and any advice given or actions advocated are solely the responsibility of the author, who assumes all liability for said work and indemnifies the publisher against any claims stemming from publication of the work.

All Rights Reserved
Copyright © 2022 by Dani Leigh

No part of this book may be reproduced or transmitted, downloaded, distributed, reverse engineered, or stored in or introduced into any information storage and retrieval system, in any form or by any means, including photocopying and recording, whether electronic or mechanical, now known or hereinafter invented without permission in writing from the publisher.

Dorrance Publishing Co
585 Alpha Drive
Suite 103
Pittsburgh, PA 15238
Visit our website at *www.dorrancebookstore.com*

ISBN: 978-1-6853-7471-6
eISBN: 978-1-6853-7610-9

Intro

Devil In Disguise

He is a Predator
He is the worst of the worst.
He treats women like prey.
He makes you feel like he's your everything, he's amazing and wonderful.
He'll get you thinking, I'm not just happy I'm over the moon elated.
And then you'll be thinking, this is too good to be true…
and it was.
In reality, he doesn't care about you at all, his main objective is to lie, steal, and destroy.
How could he care when before we met, he was already with two other women? The first one was his employee and the second one he found on Match, then me on E-harmony.
As I write these words, I am sickened.
He's a thrill seeker who tries to see what he can get away with.
He is an awful, terrible person.
He is a narcissist.
He is a sociopath.
He will get you to fall head-over-heels in love for him,
While sleeping with another woman the very next day.
Stay away from him,
He isn't just an enemy…
He is the DEVIL in disguise.

This is my story,
And THIS is brutal…

Chapter 1: 2018

Heaven

When we first met...

When we first met, I fell head-over-heels for him. We met November 23rd, 2017. So, all our first dates were Christmas-themed. Anyone who knows me just a little, knows I absolutely LOVE Christmas, to the point where I decorate the day after Halloween. I just put up my tree but…yes, I am one of those. I learned long ago to do what makes me happy. So, if it brings me happiness, I do it.

One of our first dates was putting up his twelve-foot Christmas tree on December 11th, the day he asked me to be his girlfriend. I was beginning to fall for him. He was so sweet and so charming. He knew exactly what to say and do, and he swept me off my feet, against my better judgment.

In the beginning, I did not really care. I was just coming off a bad breakup, so I wasn't really ready at all. I wasn't really over my ex-fiancé. We had broken up six months before, which was one of my first mistakes and something I'll do differently. I finally ended it with my ex-fiancé October 26^{th,} and I met Eric on November 23rd. (His birthday).

I've heard this advice before, but I never really understood it until now… Stay Single!

For at least six months to a year!

No, I don't mean date, but don't get serious.

No, stay single.

Date yourself, love yourself.

Treat yourself the way you want someone else to treat you. If you do not love yourself the way you want to be loved, then how do you expect someone else to?

Lead by example they say. No different with how you want to be treated.

I was nowhere near ready, and still very hurt by what happened with my ex-fiancé. Which made Eric come flying to me. He chased and he pursued me. He did everything I'd want a man to do. But eventually I fell, over the moon in love. I actually thought God sent him to me, because I, too, thought everything was happening too fast, but instead of fighting it, I let my guard down and let him sweep me away.

In my whole forty years, I had never loved someone the way I loved him, and still today I pray that whatever spirit that has his grip on him will release him and he will become the man he could be—a good, amazing, and loving man. With God all things are possible. It may never happen, let's be honest, it will probably NEVER happen. Something has to change deep inside him; until then or if it ever happens, I pray for whatever woman he has right now, how many there may be. I know the spell and charm he puts on and how devastating it is when you realize it was all a big lie.

My advice to any woman or man out there. If you feel something that is not quite right. You question and the internal nagging still does not go away. TRUST your instincts. Trust your gut. Trust the red flags. They do not lie. People don't change. Not unless they truly want too and are willing to do the work, which sometimes takes a lot of work.

Move on.

You will be happier.

Even if you're alone.

In the beginning

In the beginning everything was so amazing. He was amazing. I was so happy. I felt that every day with him was cause for a celebration. He was my favorite person. He was my world. The best thing that ever happened to me. I kept saying, "Somebody pinch me, this is too good to be true, I must be dreaming."

And a year later I found out it was.

We met on E-harmony. We started talking on Thanksgiving. November 2017. Which was his birthday. We texted all day long. He was sweet and charming and funny. I enjoyed our conversation. He talked about how we had matched five years earlier and wished he met me sooner and would have caused a lot less heartache.

He wanted to call me the very next day, at first that freaked me out a bit. "Who wants to call and talk on the phone these days?" I thought to myself. But that was exactly what I want. Someone who wants to talk to me, to get to know me, to show up for me, pursue me and put some effort into me. He called me right before I was playing volleyball. We made a date to meet Monday for lunch for our first date at Seasons 52.

I sat out front of the building of Seasons 52 to wait for him and as I was waiting for him; I watched a tall, very handsome, well dressed, with dark hair and glasses, and not the goofy glasses, but sleek and sexy glasses, man walk in. He had a lazy right eye, yet I found him very handsome and attractive. We sat down and had a great conversation. I was so nervous, though. When we were done, we walked out, walked me to my car, and I watched him get into his baby blue Maserati. I about died. I was like, well crap, there goes that one. He has too nice of a car. Men like that only want one thing. I told my friend, Audrey, and she said, "Run!"

I SHOULD HAVE RUN!

Yet, we kept talking. He was sweet and considerate. Sent me good morning texts and songs that I thought were so sweet and thoughtful and I loved it. We met the very next day for lunch again because he was leaving the next day to go visit his mom and brother for the holiday and their birthdays. We met at the mall this time. We had a very nice date. We ate lunch and walked around a little bit. He walked me back to my car and he looked inside and noticed that I had a scripture on my dashboard that says, "With God all things are possible." He commented on it and liked that I had that on there. Then he kissed me, our very first kiss. Which, even then I thought was way over the top, almost desperate. He nearly choked me. I literally had to wipe slobber off my chin. Yuck. Thinking back on this memory is unnerving. This probably should have been a red flag.

We said goodbye and I said, "I know you're with your family, so I'll just talk to you when you get back, don't worry about me."

Yet he was in constant contact with me the whole time.

The night he asked me to be his girlfriend.
December 11, 2017

We were putting up his twelve-foot. Christmas Tree, and let me tell you, I was nothing short of being in awe. This was the first time I went to his house. As I approached his door, there had to be at least a dozen poinsettias by his door, and he actually had Christmas lights and decorations outside. I was amazed. I rang the doorbell, and the man of my dreams opened the door. I walked into an amazingly nice, big and beautiful house. Very neat, clean, organized, and well decorated. I loved every bit of it. It was as beautiful as he was. I had made us "Christmosas" to drink and he made us an amazing dinner. As we sat at the dinner table; he asked me to be his girlfriend by saying, "Will you be my girlfriend? You're such a great catch, I have to lock it down." At first, I thought it was funny; now I think it may have been a red flag. "Have to lock it down," so no one else could catch me?

We then worked on his Christmas tree. He set up the tree. As I put up the ornaments, he set up the Christmas train that went around the tree.

Needless to say, I fell so hard. I mean a twelve-foot Christmas tree!

An Amazing man:

Successful.

Handsome.

Sweet.

Fun.

Funny.

And THIS man wanted, pursued, and said he loved me!?!??

I was in Heaven. He got me. I gave him his first Christmas present. A lit holiday house that he put under his Christmas tree. I was going to get one of those for him every year and start a collection.

Yet two days later he took down all those ornaments and the train and put it BACK up with Jill and her seventeen-year-old daughter. THEY put up the ornaments together while her daughter put the train together

So heartbreaking to find out the truth of such a wonderful time I had with him.

The hurt and betrayal.

You just cannot even imagine my pain.

Who does that????

HOW can someone DO that!??!

I just don't understand, and I may never understand.

What I do understand now is that bad people do live in this world, and that is a terrible realization to come to when you're forty. I pretty much thought everyone was basically good. Nope. Wrong. But it is a good lesson to learn.

Hallmark Christmas Movie

I felt like the star of a Hallmark Christmas movie. We had so many Christmas first dates. The botanical gardens, Christmas on 3rd, when we put up his Christmas tree, making Christmas cookies with my boys, and Christmas, just to name a few. Playing Christmas music every time Eric and I we were together.

I took him to the botanical gardens for my birthday. I go there every year and that year I took him. First, we went to dinner at Rosedale, an Italian Restaurant, which was amazing. Then we went to the gardens, and we had a wonderful time. Walking around with a glass of wine. That's where I took our first selfie together and posted it on Facebook. So many people were commenting and saying how happy I looked. But one of the Facebook friends knew the woman he worked with that he was dating (and wasn't supposed to be dating because she was his employee) had mentioned it to her about the picture. So, she had known about me earlier, but he told her we were just friends.

Christmas on third we walked around, enjoying every minute of it, but I remember him looking over at me and staring at me. I felt it a bit awkward and made me feel a little uncomfortable, but I thought that he just must really like me a lot. We ran into one of my friends and even she commented on how much he stared at me. Looking back now it was very creepy.

He went to go see his family in Minnesota in November. His mom and brother. I told him not to worry about me and spend time with his family, but he stayed in constant contact with me. I'm assuming he was doing the same with the other two.

He went to go see his dad and family in New York and his friends in Delaware, who I met later.

I had my birthday party on December 16th. I asked if it was too late to call at twelve and he said it wasn't, so we talked, always talked and always had good conversation (in the beginning). One of the friends was in the background and said, "Hi, Danielle, we can't wait to meet you." Eric made a comment, "I don't know what you did to me." So he told his friends all about ME and no one else. But why "ME" the third one in and why wait for months dating the two others and not say anything, but he just starts seeing me for only a few weeks and tells them about me?

When the truth finally came out, it was all so confusing and devastating.

On my birthday, December 22, 2017, I was taking the boys up to Orlando to go to Universal. One of the coworkers, the one that knew Kathy (girl number 1), contacted me over Facebook and told me to call her. She told me that Eric was still married. She knew I had already been really hurt and didn't want to see me get hurt again. Boy, do I wish I would have listened to her and run then. I was really upset she had to tell me that on my birthday and as I'm driving up to Orlando with my kids for our Christmas getaway. I really tried to just have a great day with my kids at Universal and we did. I was just pretty upset all day. Later that evening I spoke with Eric about it and he said yes, he was married, but they were getting a divorce.

Their marriage and whole relationship didn't last long, only lasted not even a year. Of course, he blamed everything on her, that she went crazy on him, they got in a huge fight, broken glass, cops called and everything, restraining orders on each other, etc. Of course, he told me she was cheating on him, but none of the stories ever made complete sense. He always put the blame on others when he was the one probably cheating on her all along and was the one to blame. He was really good at reeling you back in. He took the time, to explain and make sure you were okay. He always showed up. Always tried. One of the good qualities (I thought) I liked about him. Only it was just part of the excitement to him, he just liked the challenge.

Now it's Christmas. I was coming over to his house for the evening. He was "supposedly" at his families on the East Coast (who I never met, nor knew). He was going to let me know when he was back. So, I waited and waited and waited. I even called my friend Audrey, talking to her about "how long does one stay at families houses!" Especially when you have someone waiting for you. I'm normally two to three hours and then done, but all day and night, when you're planning on your girlfriend coming over seems a bit much! I started to get upset, wondering where he was.

It was about nine when I finally ended up there. Even though it was late, we ended up having an amazing evening. We stayed up until one just talking for five hours straight. It was one of the many best nights I had with him. I had got him a big picture of the New York City bridge, and he got me this card with three different getaway vacations to choose from and I LOVED that SO much! It's like he knew me so well and knew I liked to spend time together, making memories. I always had the best time with him.

I later found out that he was at Jill's house with her and her kids that morning; I'm assuming he went to Kathy's in the afternoon and then back to Jill's house that evening and then met me that night. When I spoke with Jill (after all the truth came out) she said he came to her place in the morning, left and then came back to her place that evening and was really upset he was leaving that night. She said, "Really, you're leaving us on Christmas night?"

I would have been pissed.

He was so good at coming up with excuses and reeling you back in. He was definitely on top of his game.

I'm still in shock of how deceiving one person can be.

When I was looking around at his house (a year later) when I was trying to find something on Kathy, when she contacted me. I found the same Christmas card he gave me, blank. So, I'm assuming he bought several of the same ones to give to everyone.

Sickening.

Deceitful.

Devastating.

The Rolex 24 Race

We went up to Daytona for the weekend in January 2018. First, we went up to Orlando and stayed at the universal studio hotel. We went to city walk for drinks and dancing. We had an amazing time. That is when he took my ring finger and just stared at it, holding it. And the song "Ain't Nobody" by Chaka Khan came on and he said he loved that song and that it was one of his favorites. I downloaded it and set it for his ring tone, because at the time I loved it too and it seemed just right for him. "Ain't nobody love me better than you." He was so sweet. He brought roses to the hotel and put rose petals on the bed. He was a true romantic. And I was falling for him every day. He made it so easy to love him.

From there we went up to Daytona for the races, and I met his good friends that lived close by there. Racing is not really my thing, but I enjoyed every second with him. He made every moment with him magical, no matter what we were doing. He was so attentive and focused on me. Everything he did was for me and made sure I had a great time.

Valentine's Day 2018
Our first Valentine's Day together

I woke up that morning, got ready for the day. Opened up the door to leave and there stood two dozen roses, three giant balloons, a card and rose petals all around the vase. It was amazing and such a wonderful surprise! I've never been treated like this in my life! I was so beyond happy! Over the moon elated.

On cloud nine. I was finally being treated the way I deserved. My love for him grew every day.

That evening we went to the Japanese steakhouse with my kids and I invited some good friends of mine Jon and Audrey and a couple of newly single ladies, Susan and Cindy. All very good friends of mine. I asked him if he would mind if I invited a girlfriend who just had a bad breakup and another friend who had lost her husband and I didn't want them to be alone on Valentine's Day. He didn't mind, in fact he said that amazed him and said it said a lot about who I was as a human being; kind and selfless. He said most woman wouldn't do that for Valentine's Day and would have wanted to be alone.

I had my boys give each woman a gift as their dates. The look on both their faces was priceless as one gave flowers and one gave a gratitude book. Eric paid for mine and the boys' dinner, which I never expected him to pay for all of ours, but I thought it was very sweet of him that he did.

That evening, though, he said he had to go up to Sarasota for work classes the next day. Normally, I would have thought nothing of it, but I found out that he went to Jill's that night to be with her. And had roses for her for Valentine's Day too.

Crushing to realize you weren't that special at all.

Work trips were always his excuse to be with the other girls. Later, I began to wonder, how many trainings and meetings do branch managers of banks really do?

If I had been that girl, him coming over at nine or ten, I'd have been pissed and would have known something wasn't right. I wished he would have done that to me so I would have left a lot sooner. But like I said, he was very good at reeling you back in. His persuasion was elite.

But next Valentine's Day. That was me.

Our first trip to New York
March 1st–4th, 2018

He took me up to New York for my very first time. I was in Heaven. I was in awe. I have wanted to go to New York for a very long time.

We flew into Atlantic City, New Jersey and stayed at a hotel on the boardwalk. We arrived late, but since I had never been there, we walked around the casinos. We had a great time. The next morning, I looked out the window of our hotel and noticed what a great view we had over the water and boardwalk. It was magical and amazing. Before we left for New York we walked down the boardwalk and checked the scenery and shops. Although it was very windy and nearly blew me over, every moment with him was amazing.

On our way to New York, it started snowing. I've seen snow a thousand times since I'm from Iowa, but this time, going into New York was more magical. Just being with him was magic. Just writing about it now makes me miss all the trips and fun we had.

We got into New York, at his dad's place and sure enough a nor'easter had come in and they were shutting down the roads. Since I really wanted to go, it didn't stop us from getting to the Staten Island Ferry and taking the boat into the city. We went to the museum of art and St. Patrick's Cathedral (my favorite). That was amazing, breathtaking and amazing. It was cold but so worth it! Then when we came back, we stopped at his favorite pizza place on the island.

The next morning, we got up and we got some New York bagels. Then we drove into the city. That was so cool just driving there. We went to the Brooklyn Bridge park first; it was really cool walking around there; then we went towards downtown Manhattan. I trusted him so much. I knew he was a good driver and I trusted him as we drove in the busiest, biggest city in the country. He even drove down a road backwards just to get a parking spot. Now I know why New Yorkers are known to be loud and rude; they kind of have to be like that. And I kind of liked that.

We went to Central Park because that was the one place I wanted to see. We took the subway everywhere, that was quite the experience. Ate more pizza, saw all the sights, all the tall buildings, all the people and the business. It was quite overwhelming, but I loved every minute of it! I was in awe the whole time.

We went to go visit his friend that lives in a suite in Manhattan one evening. He seemed nice. That was interesting. The next day we took the ferry back into town and spent our last day there. Just walking around there was amazing. And of course, magical just being with him.

He really knew how to sweep me off my feet!
I guess the harder you fall,
The harder it hurts
And harder it is to get over…
I just wish I could and would
Get over him sooner and faster.
And I hope someday I'll be able to love and trust again.
I hope he didn't take everything away from me,
And I hope someday, I'll feel that way again.

His dad gets sick

At the end of March, right round Easter. His dad fell and went into a diabetic coma. Eric called me from work, frantic, saying he's booking a flight to New York right away and asked me where I was, because he wanted to meet me to say goodbye. I was on my way home from work, so we met on the side of the road. He was not doing well, and I felt horrible for him. I wanted to be there for him. I offered to get a ticket to come up just to support him and be there for him, but he didn't want me to go.

Since I couldn't be there for him, the next best thing I could think of was to send him a care package. I had the boys make get well cards for him, they even wrote in there; Go Jets, because he was a Jets fan, which is funny because Michael is a die-hard Dolphins fan. I got his dad a card and an angel figurine and Eric some Easter candy, a card and a sentimental pocket pendant. When his dad got better, he sent the boys back a letter thanking them, that he is okay now and gave them $20 for ice cream. Which we later used that with Eric for all of us to get ice cream. Eric wanted to keep the letters because he never got letters like that from him. When I was there in August, his dad told me he now has a Guardian Angel watching over him and keeps it on his nightstand. I was so happy to hear he liked it and kept it near him.

Apparently, he asked the second girl to come up with him…all the while, I wanted to be there for him and she couldn't because of work. She is a nurse so I'm sure he wanted her up there to help him with the hospital and other nurses. It was all about him and what he could get out of each one of us.

Crushing…of course he denied saying any of that. He denied a lot of things, that I don't believe at all anymore…I'd believe the other women over him any day. Why would they lie to me anyways? We were all duped by him.

He's the most selfish person I know.

June. My trip to Iowa/His trip to Delaware/New York

I took my yearly trip to Iowa in June. My dad pays for our trips and Eric and I got into a fight because I didn't ask him to go, although I wanted him to go and would have loved for him to be there. I couldn't afford to get him a ticket and I was too embarrassed to ask him to go, but you'll have to buy your own ticket. Would have been very awkward and uncomfortable. I wanted hm to come up with me, but he didn't. Instead, he went up to New York and Delaware. He was helping his friend in Delaware redo his bathroom and help do some stuff around his house. Then he supposedly went to see his dad. Although when we were there in August his stepmom told me he didn't come up in June. So, I wonder if he brought or had another woman fly in to meet him in New York. It surely wouldn't surprise me. It would have had to be a different girl, as the other two women said they never went anywhere like that with him. But I'm sure there was probably more than just us three from time to time.

Second trip to New York/ New Jersey/ Delaware
August 2018

He took me back to New York to meet his family in New York and friends in Delaware. I was wondering if I should be going anyways because I was moving into my new place the next month, but it was just what we needed as a couple because we weren't doing too great. I had wanted to move in with him and was wanting to spend more time with him. We were fighting a little bit because of that. But the trip was exactly what I needed and what we needed.

We flew into New Jersey first and went to see one of my friends, Susan, who was staying there for the summer. We stayed with her the first night. We all went to breakfast the next morning. Then we headed towards Delaware, but he made a detour into Philadelphia. I had never been there before, and he wanted to surprise me. He brought me to the museum of art where the Rocky statue is and walked around the park there. It was so nice. Then we went to one of the famous Cheesesteak places, Gino's or Pat's. I can't remember, but it was really good, and I had him take a picture of me with the other places cup in front of the other shop. That was hilarious. We always had a good time joking around, laughing, talking, and having fun. Together was my favorite place to be.

From there we went to his friend's house in Delaware. We were staying there the next two nights. They had three children; one was a baby. I love kids, especially babies. The baby went right to me, and the parents were so thrilled and shocked because she doesn't go to anyone, including her grandparents. I had a great time playing with all three of the kids. They were all so adorable. The next day we went to the Delaware beaches. I really got along with the wife. She was so sweet. I really loved the whole family and I loved Delaware.

Eric and I went to Bethany beach afterwards, the one with the boardwalk later that afternoon. That was so nice and so cool. They had a band playing there as well. We stopped to watch. We had such a nice time walking down the boardwalk, looking at all the shops, getting the famous fries, walking down to the beach. Everything was amazing. The beach, the walk, the drive the talk. Delaware.

The next day we headed on up to New York to meet his dad and family. They had a surprise party for us with all of his family there to meet me. Everything was set up outside and everyone was so nice and friendly. I liked everyone, especially his dad. He was so funny. I see where Eric got his humor from. We stayed there two more days. I enjoyed talking with his dad. He was an ex–New York Police officer. We had some good conversations. I'm sure that guy has seen way too much.

But his stepmom made a comment that he wasn't up there in June when I was up in Iowa. He told me he came up here to visit his dad. Now I wonder if he even really did go and that was all a lie or if he brought up a different girl. I learned that trip as well, that his dad and stepmom didn't know that we came up there in March, when Eric told me they knew. He always withheld the truth. There was always something off with him. A lot of things never really added up.

Having several girlfriends will do that to you.

In September my lease was up and I was having to move out of my place I was renting and I had wanted to move in with him, everything was going great and I thought we were heading in that direction and I thought he wanted me to move in with previous conversations and hints that he wanted me too.

We had the conversation about me moving in with him, but he didn't want me to move in with him yet. We got in a bit of a fight because of it. He always gave hints to things like that and marriage, but he never did really mean any of it when he had two other girlfriends on the side…

Yet he got a rental truck for me and helped me move into my place. Then bought me a new/used kitchen table, saying when I moved in with him, we'd give this table to his mom when she moved to Florida.

I still have that table.

He was always making comments hinting about marriage too. One time he was holding my ring finger and asked what my ring size was. Talked about colors and where we would have a wedding. You'd see why I thought we were ready to move in together. But the plan was I move in with him when this new lease came up in a year. Guess it gave him more time to figure out what he was going to do with the other two girls…or more time to play.'

At that time, we weren't doing too good and because of that, he booked us tickets to go to New York in August for the second time…which made everything better again.

Then his birthday, my birthday, and Christmas in New York…all those… I fell so hard.

I fell in love with a bunch of lies covered by bliss…never again.

Family Pictures and time spent with my kids

In October, I was getting our annual family pictures done and since he had been a big part of our lives and I was assuming he would be in our lives for a long time I asked him if he wanted to be a part of our pictures.

We went to Riverside Park that time and we got family pictures and couples photos done.

I had canvas pictures blown up of the family and put them on my wall.

I was so angry when I found out what he was doing. I allowed him to be a part of my family!

We had done so much with the kids. Took them to an Everblades hockey game, a couple different car races, we went to the Edison home Christmas Light event, and so much more. Even had Christmas together with them and my ex-husband and his wife. Went several places with all of us together. Coparenting.

The boys really did love him. My poor kids were so devastated when the truth came out.

All our trips to Ikea and more

One of the places I really loved going with him was Ikea. I loved our trips there. Another place I had never been, so anytime we were near an Ikea, we went. I just loved walking around with him, walking through all the rooms with him. Joking around and talking, browsing and picking up stuff for our houses. But it was like dreaming about our place together. Talking about what we liked and what we wanted.

We always had to go to the food area. We loved their food; it was the best.

Just being there with him was one of my favorite things to do.

In fact, after we broke up and he begged me back, said he'd take me anywhere I wanted to go. I decided, I'd go somewhere with him for the weekend. I said I wanted to go to Ikea because I missed going there with him. He took me to St. Pete/Clear Water Beach.

Being with him.
Being with him just made me feel like a better person. I loved who I was when I was with him. I felt safe. I felt comfortable. I felt peace. I never once got drunk when I was with him. I never felt the need to. Yes, we would have one or two glasses of wine together, but that's it. I could actually sleep in with him (I was never one to sleep in). He just "felt" like home to me.

I had never felt this way with anyone. Ever. I wanted that. I loved that.

All the times we went to church together, at his church and at mine. With the boys and without. All the times we went out on his boat. One on one and one of our first date and many times with the kids. We went out several times by Punta Gorda, Bonita beach launch, and once off Sanibel with the boys. Several times with his faster boat, with and without the boys and many times with his new pontoon.

Our favorite places to go to eat. All the times we went to go eat at the roof-top bar and restaurant in Punta Gorda and the two meatballs in a kitchen. Plus, our many times just having nice dinners at home, playing dinner radio, and dancing around the house. The many times I'd surprise him with making him dinner, set up my massage table and give him a massage with a nice card for him. I did so much for him too. Now I feel so taken advantage of. So many fantastic memories, destroyed. Going to the old soul brewery after I was done playing volleyball. The times he came to visit me and watched me play volleyball. The times we played volleyball with the kids outside and going to his pool, with and without the boys. The one time we went to play pool at his clubhouse…where he put his phone in his pocket, even while playing music. He always hid his phone. I did think that was pretty suspicious.

The first major red flags.
One night, months after we were together, I came over and went upstairs and noticed ALL of our pictures were off the dressers. Not only that, the book and cards I had got him for Valentine's Day, that he normally has on his desk, were gone and my toothbrush was gone! He was so quick to excuses and always

came up with something good and somewhat believable. He had said he was taking the pictures out to copy them and the toothbrush he threw away because he had had ants on the counter and wanted to clean the counter. I should have known right then he was lying and walked away, but I don't think I really wanted to and wanted to believe him.

Another evening was a Friday night and he claimed he had to work late. I never believed that for a second! What banker works that late on a Friday night, till after nine? Actually, what banker works till nine on any night? He never wanted me to come over afterwards either. Which on Fridays, I played volleyball until eight, and usually I didn't get to his house until 8:30–9, and then we'd often go to his favorite brewery.

I should have known then that he was a lying, cheating prick and believed those red flags from the beginning. He was always too good at reeling you back in. He always came running the very next day to make everything better. I always really liked that about him. Thought he actually cared and really wanted it to work. But I was oh so wrong. He never cared at all. He was just a big man-child playing games.

Thanksgiving/His Birthday Getaway

Thanksgiving 2018 was an amazingly great day. He made everything and wouldn't even let me help. He cooked for me and the kids. He made everything that a traditional Thanksgiving has and it was very yummy.

He made the table very nice for the four of us, my kids, him, and me. We all had a very nice time. He was always very nice to my kids and they loved them.

Later that day we all played the Wii U together and then I took the kids to their dad's. I had always expected to come back to spend the rest of Thanksgiving with him, but I couldn't because he had to work on "work stuff." Between his job at the bank and his starting a new realty company with his brother and getting his reality license, he was always busy working on something. Although, now looking back, I'm not sure that he was even doing any of that and I'm not even sure he really got his realty license. It was probably a lie to get him time with the other girls.

I was a bit upset that I wouldn't be able to come over that evening. "Who works on Thanksgiving if they don't have to?" So, I went home and did my own thing, not that I minded it at all. I spoke with my biological dad that evening and he told me for the first time that he had cancer for the last six months but didn't want to tell me so I didn't panic or get upset. He went through all the chemo and the cancer is gone now. So, it ended being good news. But when we got off the phone around 9:00 p.m., I really wanted to talk to Eric desperately so I called and called and called. He never got back to me until after an hour. He said he was away from his phone, doing stuff, like he always said when I couldn't get ahold of him.

But we talked for an hour and everything was fine again. He always found a way to make up for everything and make everything better again. It was like something he got off on.

I later found out he took the leftovers to Kathy's place that night and stayed with her. In the morning she took him to drop him off at the rental car that I paid for, for his birthday getaway. He told her he was going to the East Coast to see family for his birthday.

Eric's Birthday Getaway

The next day was his birthday and I was bringing him up to St. Augustine for his birthday.

I went above and beyond. I wanted to show him how much I loved him and how I felt about him. I planned every detail step by step, by writing little love notes throughout the trip to give him clues to where we were going. Our first stop was the lighthouse. I gave him a love note about finding our love through the lighthouse. We walked up the lighthouse and had a picnic out there. Then we checked into the Casa Monica, which was one of the nicest and most expensive hotels that was right in the middle of the historic district. It was AMAZING, our room looked over the Lightner Museum. It was a beautiful, spacious suite. We even got served champagne in the lobby while we waited for our room. You really felt like royalty staying there. It was beautiful. After we checked into our room, we walked around the historic district and walked on the Loins Bridge at sunset. That was beautiful.

We came back to the hotel and got ready for the evening. I wore this really sexy slim fitting, short, gold/white dress. I think I always shocked him. I had made arrangements with his best friend that lived close by, the ones we went to the 24 Rolex Race with, for a surprise. We went down to the hotels bar and were having a drink and that was when they came up to the table and the look on Eric's face was priceless. He was so surprised and happy. I'll never forget when he turned and looked at me and said, "I have the best girlfriend ever." I replied, "You deserve it, you deserve to be treated well too and I want to show you how much I love you." I didn't make a lot of money, and I had struggled. So, pulling this trip off was something big for me, but I really wanted to do something special for him to show him how much I loved him. And at the time I thought he deserved it.

Not realizing he had two other girls on the side.

We all went out to eat. We had a great night. Later that night, I got something special for him to wear in the bedroom for him. He was very pleased.

I spoiled this man, and he didn't deserve me at all.

The next day we walked around some more and went on and off the trolley around the town. Of course, I had to stop at the winery. And one of the stops was "The kissing tree."

So, after the trolley trip was over, he just had to go back there before we left so we could kiss under that tree.

Legend has it whoever kisses under that tree will stay together forever.

Not.

Fuck that.

Legend broken, leave it to Eric to break promises.

My dream was we would go back there to get married someday.

Everything was so magical there with him.

I still can't believe what he did.

Met the family/Minnesota/Iowa

November 8th–12th we went up to Minnesota to meet his family for his mom's and brother's birthdays.

The first thing we did was go meet his mom at her work and then went to her place for a bit and then we went to his brother's, where we were staying while we were there.

He asked me since we were close to my family in Iowa, if I wanted to meet them halfway so he could meet them too. I thought that was so sweet knowing I love my family and I'd want him to meet them as well, but I wouldn't have asked because I wouldn't have wanted to take Eric away from his family.

So, my family drove up two hours and we drove down two hours just for a dinner. I have a big family so three cars were coming up in a snowstorm. My mom and dad, all three of my sisters, Darcie, Becca, and Liz and my two nieces and Becca's wife Mellany and Asher.

We had a great dinner. Everyone loved Eric. Everyone always loved Eric. He seemed like such a great guy.

The next day we went to the Mall of America. We had a great time. I had never been there before. And right around Christmas, it was like a giant Christmas wonderland for me! It was magical and amazing. We walked around and met his mother there. His mom was really nice. I really liked her a lot. We were going there to meet his brother and family there too, to go to the Japanese steakhouse for hibachi for their birthday dinners. As we were walking around, I could feel my stomach starting to hurt. I get these awful stomach pains every once in a while. Normally they don't get that bad anymore, but this time, as we were eating dinner, they got so bad I started crying at the dinner table because the pain got so excruciating. I had to leave the table at one time. It was awful and I felt awful that it got so bad. We went back to his brother's house, where we were staying and I went right to sleep. That is the only thing that will calm my stomach when it acts up that bad. It is like having a knife being cut into my side and the pain comes in waves, like contractions. It's awful.

He went out with his brother for drinks, even though he didn't want to, but I told him he needed to spend time with his brother and I'll be okay. His brother and family were not pleasant to me or us in general. He wasn't mean, but he wasn't nice. I didn't feel welcome in his house and I didn't like him too much. I don't know if my stomach flare up had anything to do with my nerves, which I think it did. I'm thinking his brother probably knew what he was doing and didn't approve of it and didn't want to get close to me because of it. It was very awkward staying there. But now I have a suspicion of why he was acting the way he was.

He had to work one of the mornings there with his brother, working on the reality company they were starting together. So, he dropped me off at the mall close by and I walked around. Later we met up with his mom to go into the city to go out to eat. All in all, it was a pretty good trip.

Now a year later, everything is a heartbreak, reliving everything every day and wondering why everything happened the way it did. Wishing none of it was true. But realizing it IS true; he is never going to change, and I HAVE to move on.

My Surprise 40th Birthday Party/December 8th, 2018

My 40th birthday was approaching, and I was talking about wanting to throw a party in January, when I got back from Iowa for Christmas.

One day, I was on my way over to his house on a Saturday night. He told me to wear something nice, because his aunt and uncle were coming down and we all were going to go to dinner. So, I got ready and heading out on my way. As I'm driving a thought went through my mind, wondering if he may be throwing me a surprise party. I pull up to the house and I noticed a bunch of cars parked down the road a little bit and that thought went through my mind again. I go to the door and he opened the door and everyone yells, "Surprise!" I was shocked, surprised and elated. He couldn't have done a better job. I loved him so much and I was so happy. He was just amazing. Everything I had ever wanted. A dream come true. That was the moment I let myself fall completely and totally, head-over-heels in love with him. In my whole forty years, I never felt this way about anyone. He is it, he is the one. I'm going to marry this man. All I ever wanted. Now I was thankful that it never worked out with my ex-fiancé.

He planned an amazing birthday party for me. Had all of my best friends there, my ex-husband, his wife, and my kids were all there. He had food, cake, music, games, alcohol galore. He even put the projector outside with the movie *This is 40* on and a giant Jenga game.

He even had my sisters call in at the same time over Facebook video chat and put it on the big TV so they all could wish me a happy birthday! It was the coolest! He was always the best.

It was amazing. He was amazing. All of my friends were amazed. We were all smitten by his charm. It was the best time and that was the time I finally let all my walls down and fell completely for him. All those doubts I had before, I just put away. I thought what man would be cheating on me and do all this for me? I just didn't think it was possible. I was so in love.

But I was wrong.

In fact. after finding out and talking to all of my friends, they were saying how every time someone would call saying someone was at the gate and they asked if it was me, he said it wasn't. And they said he was acting so nervous, thinking he was so nervous about me coming and wanting everything to be great. But really it was the other girl trying to get through the gate at the same time I was coming through the gate.

She was calling and texting nonstop. Later that night, I went looking for him and he was nowhere to be found. When I found him, he came walking around the outside of the house from the neighbor's house saying he was putting chairs away, but I know he was talking to her.

What is worse, is that night I finally let my guard down totally. I finally decided to fall completely and totally in love with him, a year later and after everything we'd been through. Through suspicions, and some red flags, and some trials, I decided that anyone who could do this, must truly love only me and want only me.

I was so very wrong.

Come to find out soon after; he went to Kathy's house the very next night.

How can someone do that?

How can someone be so heartless?

It's so heartbreaking to let someone fall head-over-heels for you, then sleep with another woman the VERY NEXT day!

What? Like I was nothing. I don't get how someone can do something like that for someone, then turn around and be with another woman?

I'm beginning to realize he never really loved me at all.

But I can love myself the way he did, but didn't.

I'll do everything he did for me.

Everything I miss about him; I'll do for myself.

I'm not lonely, I'm just alone.

And that's okay.

When my world came crashing down.
Christmas 2018

We were going to New York for Christmas! To see his family and for me to see Christmas in New York, which was #1 on my bucket list. We were going to see the big Christmas tree at Rockefeller Center! I was so excited. The big Christmas tree, the huge nutcrackers, the ice skaters, the huge sculptures, the lights, Sacs off 5th's display of lights. It was ALL SO AMAZING and breathtaking!

I really thought he was going to propose to me. All my friends thought he was going to propose to me. I thought, "this is it!" This will be my time. What better place than New York, in front of that tree, to a girl who loves Christmas?

We were going to be staying at a hotel in downtown Manhattan. He was taking me to the Rockettes show the very next morning. I thought he'd propose that night, because why get a room when your dad lives in Staten Island.

But he didn't. So, I thought, at the show, he'll propose to me at the show. But he didn't.

At the Rockettes show, we sat in the 6th row back. That show was amazing and I was in awe that whole show. I almost cried because no one had ever done so much for me. I caught him just staring at me, I thought he was just admiring how happy I was. And I was in awe of him, of us, and I was just so happy and so in love.

That afternoon we went to his family's Christmas. Which was a lot of fun. There were Christmas cookies, Christmas food, laughter, cheer, and drinks galore.

They were all great, fun, and funny. I really enjoyed my time meeting them and being a part of his family for Christmas. I really loved his family.

We had a magical and amazing time. The whole trip was amazing.

I thought maybe he'd propose to me with all his family there. I really thought he'd ask me to marry him at some point through that trip. He kept giving me hints and everything, but nope, he didn't propose to me. Instead of a proposal, I got a Facebook message from his other girlfriend, saying she's been with Eric for a year and a half.

That's when my world came crashing down.

That when my world turned upside down.

I was so crushed and confused.

I didn't believe her at first. In fact, no one could believe it. My first response to her was, "How is this possible? I'm with him all the time and even if I'm not with him, I'm on the phone with him for an hour or two every night I'm not with him." He denied it, said he dated her before he met me and she's jealous and wanted him back. So, I actually believed him and blocked her, thinking she was making it all up. He claimed she was crazy and making it all up.

Except she wasn't and there were always a few things that she said and showed me, that never made any sense to me that I couldn't stop questioning....

Chapter 2: 2019
Year of Hell

December 18th-First counseling session
We get back from New York and I am confused and feeling lost. I don't know what to think at this point. He says it wasn't true and she way lying. Even though I made myself believe that he didn't do this, had hoped and prayed it was all a lie, I started to question my trust in him and all the little to big red flags from the past.

The first thing he did was set up counseling appointments for us. I was leaving to Iowa for my family Christmas in four days. He made an urgent appointment so we could start right away. He was always good at showing up when he needed to and to make it "seem" like he was the perfect man.

We had our first counseling appointment. It was virtual over the computer at his house. I really liked our counselor, a Christian man. He listened to us and Eric allowed me to talk first and share my thoughts and feelings. He was always so sweet and he actually seemed like he really felt bad and wanted to fix it.

I was heartbroken but hopeful.

December 19th–Journal entry
I'm confused, I have unanswered questions. I don't know what to do and how to process all of these emotions. Thinking of the possibility of you being with

another woman, sleeping with her? It hurts. I don't even want to think about that. And are these texts real? Were you just talking with her? Or was it something just in the beginning? Did you really mean all those things you said to her? How is this all possible? Thanksgiving? My birthday?

Her anniversary card…You gave her…with your writing? The "Day" Saturday? All the times you weren't around when I was trying to reach you? Were you really with her? All the trips you took. And if this is all true, can I be with you? Can I trust you again? I don't know. And can you change and never do this again and put me through this again? I can't STAND the thought of you being with someone else physically. It makes me sick to my stomach.

I want the truth.

I want answers.

I want honesty.

I want peace.

I want safety.

I want to be comforted and know that everything is going to be okay and I'll never have to feel this pain again…

*And then finding out later when I spoke with Jill, about all the messages, I "actually saw" them going back and forth about seeing each other and her wanting him to come over on Christmas Eve to make love to her and him saying yes. During Christmas while I was in Iowa, devastated, and while we were going to counseling to try and save our relationship and in constant contact with me, while his mother was there with him. He was talking with her. His ex. His friends-with-benefits girl. Disgusting.

January 26, 2019, year two: Rolex race

This year we planned on bringing my boys. I was concerned because I didn't know how we were doing as a couple. It wasn't great and we were struggling. I thought this was a chance to bring something back for us.

It was us four and his two male friends from up northern Florida. One from when we went up to St. Augustine for his birthday getaway and last year's Rolex race.

On my way to Eric's house, the boys and I got something to eat real quick. Eric got really mad at me because I didn't wait for him, but my boys eat earlier than he does. He would always get mad at me for thing like that.

We get up there and he was acting so weird. We checked into the hotel we were staying at and there were some problems getting into the rooms. When we were in our rooms finally. I was in the room with my boys and he and his friend were walking around outside talking on the phone and it upset me. That was the first indication that he was talking/seeing someone new, a brand-new girl.

The whole weekend didn't feel right. Not at all like the year before where he was trying to woo me and everything was amazing and magical. It was like I didn't even exist, and I was an afterthought. Him and his guy friends were more important than me and the boys. Last year where it was all about us and getting pictures together. He was all about them and getting guy pictures. Finally, even his friend was like, "Why don't you get a picture with her?" Eric was like, "Oh, yeah." I was an afterthought. I know he was taking pictures to send to his new girl.

Everything was awful. Heartbreaking.

February 2019—Year of Hell
One of our counseling sessions went extremely bad.

After starting our counseling appointments. In one of our counseling appointments, he was getting extremely upset and mad because I brought up some of the red flags that had happened throughout our relationship that indicated that possibly what she was saying could be true as well as the things she said that made no sense that I couldn't shake. The anniversary card that he gave her, that he said he gave to her for their five-month anniversary. But who does that? I kept asking myself, "Who does that? I don't believe it." Plus, that would mean we started dating one month later and he never did mention her at all when we had the "Ex" talk. Him missing for that hour during Thanksgiving and her saying he came to her house that evening with our leftovers. None of it made sense and I was just trying to make sense of it all.

He was so awful, and the counselor could tell he was getting upset and irritated. The counselor even said something to him, like, "this seems to upset you a lot and just take a breath." Like he knew he was being called out and he didn't like it. We were reading a couple's relationship book together, working on our relationship, as the session was ending, I was significantly afraid. I thought to myself, *please don't go*, to the counselor. It's not going to be good and I'm a little scared. When the session was over, he immediately threw the book at me and started screaming at me. Yelling so much, he was spitting in my face, calling me a slut and a whore and would come right up to me, right into my face shaking his fist at me, like he was going to hit me. Screaming so much, he was spitting in my face.

I was terrified. Devasted.

I was extremely afraid, hysterically crying and wanting to get of there. He kept throwing all of my stuff at the door, telling me to leave. I wanted to leave anyways and as I'm at the door, shaking and trembling, he kept saying, "If you leave, don't bother ever coming back." I never wanted to come back anyway, so I walked out the door, bringing nothing with me, got into my car and here he comes after me, begging me to come back in.

So, stupidly I did.

Oh, how I wish I just drove away. And never looked back.

Another mistake made. I wish I would have driven away, sped away AS soon as I got in the car and never gave him a chance to reel me back into his web of lies.

Valentine's Day 2019

Even though I found out about Kathy in December. Since I thought she was lying, we were still trying to work it out. You would think he would be worshipping the ground I walked on and trying very hard....

I took the time and made a scrapbook for him. I did that to try and help me grow closer to him and help me get over what Kathy had said. It was the second scrapbook I made for him. I made him one for Christmas of all the trips we'd taken, we had done so much I had to make another one and I thought what better time than Valentine's Day, while we were struggling. I also got him Norman Love chocolates, a stuffed animal bear and a Jesus calling book.

And he got me…a bag a roses that he just handed to me the night before Valentine's Day. No card. Nothing else! So I was hoping for something else on Valentine's Day.

The day before Valentine's Day, we all went out to dinner, with the boys. While we left, he gave me a bag of a dozen roses from Publix, still in the bag. Not in a vase, not even nice ones. Crappy roses. Normally, I'm not that judgmental and I am happy with what I get, but after everything we went through and everything that happened and what he gave me and did for me last year, I was hoping for something special…like a ring.

But nope. He was giving to someone else.

The next day his aunt and uncle from New York were visiting. We were going to be meeting up with them for dinner. I sat at Outback waiting to find out when to go over, talking with a friend of mine that worked there. I was getting very upset and impatient. It was 7:00 p.m. and I was still waiting to hear from him. I didn't get the okay to come over there until around 8:00 p.m. and didn't get there until around nine all because he was running "late."

No, he wasn't running late, he took his new girl out to dinner. Now, I'm the idiot.

The next day we all went out to dinner. You could definitely feel the tension between Eric and me. It was not pleasant.

And that weekend, we had finally planned an evening out by ourselves to go out to dinner. I bought a brand-new very nice long sexy red dress for the occasion, and we were going to one of our favorite restaurants in Punta Gorda, the rooftop and piano bar and restaurant. I came over and got ready and he just lay in bed, like he was tired and barely got up to go, as if he didn't want to. I was starting to feel like a nuisance. I couldn't believe after everything we went through; he couldn't put more effort into us.

And no other gift at all. Just those dozen crappy Publix roses. And again, not even the nice ones, they were already half-dead…like our relationship that once was so vibrant and alive and beautiful. Now is dead.

The time his brother came to visit.

His brother was coming for a visit for a long weekend. He was buying a home here in Southwest Florida. It was a Friday that he was coming in town. Eric was saying, they were going to go out just him and his brother. Which I was fine with, I was just asking to please be able to come over that evening when they got home to stay with him. I begged and pleaded that I needed to be with him, with everything that happened between us, I needed that.

No matter how much I pleaded and begged, he would not allow me to come stay with him that night. I don't believe his brother was here yet and I believe that he was with the other "new" woman.

The next morning, he came over to "reel" me back in.

That evening I went over there to watch a movie and I was instructed not to say anything to him about the night before. I was always a good girlfriend who didn't overstep any boundaries but that caused me a lot of heartache in the end.

I wish I would have stood up for myself; I wish I would have asked more questions. I guess I was afraid I'd learn the truth and deep down I didn't really want to know.

The less you know, the less it hurts. Until the end when it all comes out anyways and you're left feeling like an idiot…still left feeling the pain. Only now it's worse. Way worse.

Another New Girl

I'm not 100% sure if there was a new girl, as I have no proof, but his actions over the next few months would lead me to believe otherwise. And lead me into searching and finding the second girl in March. Now I believe 99.9% that he had another new girl in January, after I found out about Kathy, and he only had me left. I guess I wasn't enough for him, and he needed to replace Kathy with someone else.

Reasons why I believe:
The certain things that use to be normal became different. Like Saturdays, coming over and spending the day with him helping him do chores around the house, then going out to dinner. The way he treated me, became different. Everything changed. Every reason why I loved him changed. His effort was gone.

In January:
He came to my house one Friday night at twelve. I had always told him not to even bother coming over to my house if it was ten or after. And WHY was he coming over to my house at twelve? On a FRIDAY night!

He was on a date with the new girl.

One day he said he was on his way from his office, but he was in Estero and he said it would take longer to get there. I live in Bonita, which his other office in Naples, is farther away, forty-five minutes and the office in Estero is twenty minutes away. For some reason, it took him over an hour to get to my place. I believe he was either with her or talking to her on the phone. What he did to all of us apparently.

In the beginning of February:
One Thursday night, he traveled out of town for work, so he says. We always spent Thursday nights together and I had always expected I'd come over after he got back. But he kept telling me he didn't want me to come over because he was feeling sick and having stomach problems. I was saying "I don't care that you're sick; we're a couple and that stuff doesn't matter and if I was there, I could take care of you. And if eventually, I moved in, that stuff shouldn't matter."

So, I was on my way there, at this time, I could go into his place and be there without him. I could always get through his gate (so I thought). But I got stuck outside his gate and I could not get through it. I tried to call him several times and he conveniently didn't call me back till I was halfway home. I believe he was either with the other woman or she was waiting for him at his house. Or he didn't even go out of town, and he was home with her or out with her. This caused a huge fight where we almost broke up and we should have. That night he really showed me everything I really needed to know. The next day I went to play volleyball and the group of us went out dancing, while he waited for me at my house, fretting.

While I was out with my volleyball friends: Jamie, Kent, and others, I had such a blast, I love to dance and they all knew what happened with Eric, so they were trying to lift my spirits. That's why we even went out to this place, so I could dance and let loose. However, Eric tried calling my phone, over and over and over again. So much that one of my friends ended up blocking his number. That man just wouldn't stop. He was relentless.

He had got me some flowers and put I love u in flower petals on my pillow. Which I didn't remember because the volleyball people gave me WAY too many shots! These are the things he'd do to reel himself back in. And the way he talked and influenced you. He was so good at reeling back in. he should have been a fisherman. Patient and good at what he did.

End of February; The Day my World Fell Apart
I decided to look through his house.

One Thursday I was over there while he was at a HOA meeting. He was the president of the HOA. Good way for a sociopath to make sure he oversees everything and takes control.

Nothing was getting better; in fact, everything was getting worse. So, I decided to search for evidence on Kathy. Though I didn't find anything on her, I found the second girl. She had given him a card that he kept in one of his spare bedrooms on the closet floor. She had given him a Groupon for a massage no less. Thankfully it had her full name on it, so I searched for her and found her on Facebook. I pondered if I should even reach out to her. It took me a few days to work up the courage to do so. I thought, well it's not getting any better. In fact everything is getting worse, so, why would it hurt?

It was Friday March 2nd, we went to the Cornerstone Strawberry Festival and he made the remark, "This is your day, anything you want to do." It struck me off guard because we ALWAYS spent Saturday together as well. He said he had too much stuff to do Saturday and he couldn't spend the day with me. I argued with him, because I stated the fact that I always help him with his Saturday chores; why couldn't I help him with them this time? So, the next day, I finally reached out to her because I felt: "What do I have to lose at this point?"

March 3rd, 2019

So, Saturday March 3rd rolled around. He still wasn't saying if we were doing anything or not. So, I finally reached out to Jill. I first reached out to her on Facebook and asked if she knew Eric, she replied, "Yes we dated, but we stayed really good friends." At first, I was like *oh shit! He's going to know I was asking if they're still friends and they dated previously. Crap.* Then she replied when they broke up. I replied, "This past October?" I was sickened, I said, "I've been with Eric since December 2017. I was so upset. She was shocked and upset and hurt. All the emotions I had been going through. Now all three of us, felt the same way.

They were together from September 2017 to October 2018.

They had broken up beforehand, but they had stayed friends…you know the ones with benefits kind.

I can't hold anything in, and Eric was actually with me that afternoon, looking at my van, it was having some problems. And he already knew I was talking to Jill (my first indication he had access into my Facebook account, which didn't dawn on me until later because I was so distraught about what I just learned).

He admitted it. He admitted that EVERYTHING was true.

With Jill *and* Kathy. I was so horrified.

That was the day my world fell apart.

Not just a fling, not a one-night stand with either of them. Full blown Love Relationships! With all three of us! Wtf?

I called my best friend Audrey and told her what was going on and her and her boyfriend Jon, were going to the Irish Fest, so they came and picked me up. I didn't want to be alone that evening. I talked with Jill throughout the evening and Eric tried to contact me the whole evening, even though I know he still kept his plans with the new girl.

He had written a long text to both women, stating he had only wanted me and that it was always me. It was me he brought to New York, it was me he introduced to all his family and friends. It was me that he spent all his time with. It was me that he wants in his life and if I decide to keep him, he is going to whatever it takes to keep me.

I know he did this because both of them told me and texted me the messages. I felt terrible because I didn't ask him to hurt them too. It was all so bad. It was horrific. I felt terrible I didn't listen to or believe Kathy and actually thought she was being spiteful and wanted to break us up, when in all reality, she was just as hurt, and wanted to help me and I just shunned her. I later reached back out to her to apologize to her and tell her there was a third girl too. Neither of them wanted to know the other one. I think it was just too much for any of us to bare. Kathy wasn't shocked that there was another one. We talked on the phone a few times, but never met in person, but we remained friends on Facebook.

Jill told me everything. We met in person one day at a restaurant. She had told me he had asked her to go up to New York with him when his dad was sick. Of course, he denied it. He denied a lot of things. That I don't believe anymore.

I'd believe both of these women over him any day. Why would they lie to me? We were all duped by this man.

One of them told me he bought her a car. He denied it. I don't believe him.

He bought me a car too, a piece of shit car, and then made me feel bad about it. You don't buy something for someone and then make them feel bad for it.

He used me for massages. I gave him a massage every week or every other week. Sometimes I was in severe pain, giving him a massage and he knew it and still took from me. I had always wanted to be there for him and give to him, but not at my expense. One time, I overdid it and I had to cancel my whole day the next day because I hurt myself so bad.

192 Roses

Sixteen dozen roses are what he thought could make up for all of the lies and all the deceit, all the gut-wrenching pain that he had caused me.

One day about a month after we broke up, when he was begging me to get back together with him, he brought over 192 roses, sixteen dozen for every month we were together.

One of my thoughts as there were so many thoughts that were going through my head was, "Yeah, now you get me nice flowers." Now that you've been caught. Not when it was Valentine's Day and we were trying to work on our relationship. Now you try? *NOW?* Now that my heart has been torn apart. Now that he's been caught being a massive manipulator, cheater, and liar.

It was just a way to manipulate me back into his arms. And it worked for a while. We'd go back and forth for a while. I'd be good for a week or two but then the hurt and the sadness would creep in. Missing him and the sadness was way too much for me to bear. The temporary fill, even though I knew it wasn't good for me, would keep me happy for a short time, until I'd come back to reality, knowing this will never be able to work again. No matter the counseling, no matter the trying.

I thought that if he went to counseling and tried. And he did for a while. I thought that if he could change and just pick me, if I would just be good enough for him, he'd be good with just me, we could work it out. I had high hopes. I really wanted the relationship we had, and I would have done anything for it. If only I could have been enough. But I wasn't and that was not my fault. He has demons.

He told me that he'd give me access to all the cameras in the house, I can check his phone anytime I wanted, would buy me a new car, let me move in, and marry me. Everything I had ever wanted, now he was ready and wanted it. But just after finding out everything, I didn't want anything from him!

Hospital Trip

I had purchased him tickets for a Yankees game that I got for him for Christmas. The game was at the end of March. I told him after the breakup, I was still going to give him the mobile access to them, but please don't bring another woman with him. He begged me to go with him. So I went to his house that Sunday morning to get the tickets transferred and go. While I was there, he was having trouble transferring them and through what I call a man-child fit, like he sometimes did. He abruptly sat down and I heard a pop and he went immediately down, crying, down to the floor in pain. My first thought was, this is it, this is his karma and I get to watch. As I watched him lying there writhing in pain, I felt satisfaction, because this man won't be able to feel emotional pain, but physical pain, he does feel. He popped a disc in his back by throwing a fit! How fitting.

But as I sat there watching him, of course, my empathic self starts to feel bad and I waited on him hand and foot. I tried to help him get and do whatever he needed. I even gave him a massage to try and help him feel better. The poor guy just lay there on the floor in pain.

(Yeah, right, poor guy! He deserved everything he got)

He had his friend coming there to help get him to a hospital. I had told him I was going to go home and needed to do some work on my house and clean up, but after I realized how bad he was and that he was going to go to the hospital, I was wanting to go to. But he didn't want me to stay and kept trying to push me out of the house before his friend got there. Telling me that, "No, we got it and it would be weird with him being there." He was the friend that knew that he was dating two of us. But I told him, "That it didn't matter and given the circumstance, I'm sure we could all be adults." As I was leaving the gate called and he said, "No." I asked what was that all about. I was getting the feeling he had the other girl coming over too and I believe that is what happened. As I was walking out of the door, I ran into his friend, and he looked shocked to see me. I told him I wanted to help, but Eric didn't want me to help, so I'm leaving.

They went to the hospital. I told him to tell me which one he went to when he got there. He told me he was going to Health Park Hospital. The next day, I went to go visit him and he told me not to come visit, which is odd. So the next day, I started to wonder if he even went to the hospital, because he's always lying and I can't even trust anything he says anymore. So, I called Health Park to see what room he was in and they told me, he's not at this hospital, that he was at Lee Memorial Hospital. I asked, "Was he even there? Was he transferred?" Certainly, there is some reason he didn't tell me what hospital he was at. But no, he was not there at all and went straight to Lee Memorial, probably because he had his new girl there.

I flipped out when I heard he was at a different hospital and blocked him again, but somehow, he got back ahold of me by his friend.

All the signs were always there. He just had a good way of lying and denying and making you believe him. I guess I always wanted to believe him.

His mom flew down to help him. I went there to see him afterwards when he got home, he had back surgery, and we were in his room and I noticed a box of condoms in his night drawer, which he never had them there before and supposedly, he was just chasing after me? Yeah, right. All the signs were there. What was I thinking?

Sociopath, Narcissist, or Just Crazy? You decide.

*After I learned about what he did, I started to realize, little by little how crazy he was. I had to block him from Facebook, and when I looked further, I found more than thirty profiles in his name or close to his name with no picture and I had to block as well.

*Him knowing I was talking to the second girl through Facebook messenger, before I even mentioned her name.

*Later while looking through his phone (when we were talking and still trying to work it out) I saw a screenshot of a friend of mine of the opposite sex in his phone. My friend had reached out to me on Facebook messenger and asked me to go out and I replied, "No, I'm still with my boyfriend." By the way, this friend of mine is hot, hot, hot. His nickname is Hot teacher. So Eric knew I could have went my own way if I wanted to, but I was still trying to work it out with him, even with everything that happened after the first girl.

*Another day was when I blocked him and hadn't talked to him for a whole month, trying to move on. I had set a professional luncheon date with one of my networking colleagues through my email. As I was standing there waiting in line, Chad to my left, I turned to my right and there was Eric standing right next to me. I froze. I hadn't talked to him for a month, trying my hardest to move on. Of course, he wanted to talk. We walked to the side, I excused myself from Chad real quick. Eric tried to turn everything on me, asking me, "What are YOU doing here? Did you know I'd be here? I'm here to get a key made at Target." He always made a way to turn everything on me. It was a great gas lighting technique that narcissists do.

It was just another way to rope me back in and of course it worked again. Until I came back to my senses.

That's when I knew I had a problem and I needed to change all my passwords. I ended up closing my email account and opened a new one, because he wouldn't leave me alone.

*He showed up at my house unannounced and not welcome and then would not leave…and then changed my password to my lock on my front door to the one he knew.

*He showed up at my work on a Saturday afternoon. I had an afternoon appointment that I had scheduled online. I don't normally work on Saturday afternoons, and he knew that. I just know that he made that appointment because instead of her showing up, he showed up trying to get me to talk to him. This was after he went away for the weekend for a "work" trip that I didn't believe he actually went on a work trip, but a trip with his new girl. I had just got back from Iowa on a three-week summer road trip vacation. We "were" actively trying to work it out. I got back on a Thursday, in July. He came to see me that night. Friday he was heading up to Orlando for a class for Saturday morning. I didn't understand why he had to leave so early on Friday, and I had suggested to come see me before he went up there. He claimed he was stuck at work till five and then HAD to rush up there. So much bullshit. So, I actually did something I would not normally do, I called his work asking for him. They said he left early that day. So, this time I finally caught him in a lie. I believe he took the new girl somewhere. He is such a player and I'm an idiot for trying with him…so many times. And to think I would ever be enough for this man. I kept asking him why he had to go on a work trip right when I came back from a three-week vacation. Couldn't he go another time? But to realize that he went with his new girl the moment I get back? Why? So, disheartening. I was never good enough for him. Never was, never would have been. But really no one will ever be good enough for him.

*One day out to dinner with my friend Tracie, at outback, we were sitting at the bar and I got several different calls over and over from all different numbers for about an hour. Tracie was like wow! He's Psycho. I knew it was him, I just knew it. Since I blocked him, he'd try any way he possibly could to get to me. And he admitted it was him.

*All the camaras IN his house, not outside his house, inside. He said they weren't on, just a motion sensor. But he lied. Always lying. Even my friend Audrey made the comment on how creepy that is and how he probably watches back all the different women he had there, like a sociopath would.

When she was over at his place for my surprise birthday party, she mentioned to me how odd it was that there were no little mementos or pictures of us. No sign of me anywhere in his house at all.

*He went on so many weekend and weekday work trips. Which later I learned that branch managers don't do many weekend work trips, mostly weekdays and not that many. And after learning he was with two other women and went away for the weekends with them as well. Makes me sick.

He had gone to a professional work dinner event with Jill and actually had professional pictures taken with her. Met all her family, friends, and coworkers. Met all of Kathy's family. But he never introduced them to his. Jill and Kathy even knew he didn't even tell his family about them. Sometimes I wonder if they knew about me and they were side girls and fine with it. But for as devasted as they were, I don't think so. However, Kathy told me, she never wanted anything serious and actually asked him if he wanted an open relationship. Only with me, he was my everything and I wanted to marry that man.

*I was speaking with a Naples police officer I met on a dating site that I got on after I found out about everything. I know I shouldn't have been dating, but I needed to get my mind off everything, and this just helped. I met him a couple times over lunch and told him about what was happening with Eric and the stalking and stuff, and he said, "Look, Danielle, I have enough here I can press charges on him and put a restraining order on him, just say the word and

I'll do it." He even paid a visit to his branch at the bank. I just couldn't bring myself to do it, although I wish I had.

He is a bad, bad person and I wouldn't trust him as your banker either. He had asked Jill if he could be her power of attorney. Which is so scary. This man needs to stay away from women and people's money. Period.

Weekend trip to Clearwater/Tampa

After going back and forth for a while, he begged me to go on a trip together. Since I missed him terribly and our trips together—our trips to Ikea—I said yes. I wanted to go to Ikea with him at least one last time and enjoy time with him again.

We went for the weekend up to Tampa and walked around Ikea and then we went to Clearwater Beach the next day. I missed spending time with him and being with him.

During our breakup, it was so hard for me. I'd wake up so, so sad. Walking like a zombie out to get my coffee, saying to myself over and over, *I'm so sad*. Wishing I'd wake up and it was just a horrible nightmare. Asking myself how am I ever going to get through this? I didn't see any hope for myself or for my future. All I felt was this tremendous hurt and pain. I just couldn't bear it and I would cave and reach out to him. I just had a tiny hope that maybe he could change, maybe I could be okay with it…maybe. Just one more try, if I could get what I had back, it be worth it. I would go through cycles like these. And everything would be good for a week or two until I'd come to my senses and realize who he truly was and he would never change and that I would never be okay. I came to realize it would never work again.

Counseling

He was going through his own counseling. I told him he needed to work on himself. No normal person goes around doing things like this. "You need to go love yourself," I had told him. So, he was supposedly going to counseling by himself and we were starting to do counseling together before I went away for summer vacation. Which ended by the time I got back. I thought that maybe if he's in serious counseling and trying and wanting to change and work on himself. If he truly wanted only me. I'd take him back in a heartbeat. All I wanted was the relationship we had before. I wanted him back, I wanted me back, I wanted the person I was when I was with him. I liked me when I was with him.

July 2019, tried to give it another try

Even after everything that happened, I finally said we could give it another try, like REALLY try. Right before the summer road trip with my boys. I even told my family we were going to try and work it out. Told them we were going to counseling and he is trying. I loved him so much that I thought that if he could change and only be with me, I'd take him back in a second. My family was supportive, they just didn't want to see me hurt anymore.

But while I was away, a few really bad things happened and I ended up ending it before I even got home.

He tore me down pretty good, had a way of making me feel awful. He made "ME" pay for his mistakes. Classic narcissist traits.

One Wednesday, we were having a sister day with all my sisters for my sister's wedding. We went to try on our dresses, went to a winery, and then went back to my sister Liz's house to play games. We ended up getting done by seven. My mom was gone, and my kids were at their grandpa's for the evening, so it was just me and it was the perfect time for us to actually talk. The last time I texted with him was at 3:00 p.m. and I tried calling him and texting him with no response, until 11:00 p.m. that night saying he fell asleep at eight, which is bullshit because this man doesn't go to bed until eleven most nights. Even if he fell asleep at eight, why hadn't I heard from him at all since three?

There was always something wrong the whole trip. Him not picking up his phone, him going away. Every time I had enough, he would have his friend call me or text me saying, "Call me immediately." EVERY TIME I tried to break up with him and block him, he'd have his friend call or text. One time his friend texted me, "Call me back, if something happens to Eric, I'm going to blame you entirely." So, he was crying wolf to his friend and telling him he was going to kill himself and he'd call me thinking I'm the one being unreasonable and poor Eric is so hurt. But they never stopped to wonder how I was and how everything was affecting me. It was ironic because he actually made "me" feel that bad that summer that I had thoughts of killing myself. I felt so low, the lowest I felt since I was fourteen when I was raped by my first boyfriend, while he ruined my life, Eric ruined my world.

I found out while on vacation that he went through my journal. I was reading one of my many self-help books on healing and I was *actually* doing the work in it. Some of my past stories and pain and he read something in there that was for my eyes only, something that is very personal and painful part of my past, and he took it and ran with it. Knowing how hurtful it was to me; he said what I did was worse than what he did and made me feel awful. But what I did was something to myself. I NEVER ever hurt anyone else. Only myself. Again, to *myself* and in *my* past! Years before. What he did was hurtful to me, right now, in the present. I told him, "What you did was in our present and it tore everything we had apart and what you did hurt me terribly." We aren't the same. I've tried my whole life to be a good person; all you do is lie, cheat, betray, and manipulate and you actually enjoy it! What I did was out of hurt, but I never went out trying to hurt others like he did.

But he proceeded to make me feel horrible about myself, so bad I even contemplated removing myself from this world. I even talked myself into believing my boys would be better off without me. They have their dad and stepmom and they would be okay without me and everyone else would be too. While I was having actual real hurt feelings and thoughts like this, he was threatening this lie to his friend because this man is too selfish to ever actually kill himself. This was the lowest I've been since I was fourteen when I actually wanted to kill myself. I hated myself and the hell I was going through then.

Reading Session with a Professional Psychic—November 2019

After I hadn't spoken with Eric for months, I was finally getting over him. I hadn't talked to him since the incident from my summer vacation.

I was finally doing much better. Starting my self-healing journey.

I heard of a professional psychic. He was very well known and renowned psychic. He read for the famous. He was always very good, and I would hear him talk on the radio station about taking negative energy off of people. I thought there was a possibility that I had some negative energy around me that I wanted removed. It was expensive to talk to him. $500 per half hour. I thought it would be worth the $500 just for the negative energy removal alone.

So, I called him and he removed the negative energy around me and looked into Eric and me and said, that yes, there was someone, but there doesn't look like there is anyone else anymore. I told him a little bit about what happened and he said, I can't even believe I'm saying this, but I'm hearing that you should go back to him. That he misses you and can change and wants you back. That it has always been you.

I was so distraught; I didn't know what to do. I had finally gotten over him. I was on my way to getting better! I had totally removed him from my life and I didn't know how to even get a hold of him. But found his number in my blocked contacts and I texted him…again. Heart sinks.

He, of course, gets back to me immediately and we start talking again and seeing each other. But it is still not good. We met at Gulf Coast Town Center on a Monday evening for dinner to talk, and then on a Saturday to walk around and when he left in his car, I saw him on his phone and I swore he blew a kiss to someone and I said something to him. And he said he didn't do that. But I know what I saw.

This time I wasn't able to come over on Thursdays or any day at that. He was wanting to come over during the day instead of seeing me at night. I got suspicious and ended up going over to his house on a Saturday. I kept asking him what he was doing and to let me know when he was ready to do something. After putting me off, I just ended up driving over there. He did end up letting me in the house, but it took a while for him to answer the door and he came to the door and he was sitting down eating a pot roast that was cooking. I was irritated because he never told me he was making something. He made an excuse that I couldn't stay and made me leave. He ended up coming over that night but ended up leaving very early the next morning, which I thought was weird. He just wanted to come over during the day. And I felt like that was a red flag.

We ended up going to the botanical gardens together for the night of lights for Christmas. I love going there every year, and I thought it would be nice if we went. I was hoping we would go out for dinner first or after but no, he only had time to go to the gardens because his mom and brother were here for Christmas—of which I have so many suspicions.

I had been trying to reach the second girl. I stayed in contact with both girls. I didn't hear from her for Thanksgiving. I sent a Happy Thanksgiving to her with no reply, which I thought was odd. So, I sent another message after I had been with Eric for a while, just saying hi and hoping she was okay and I wanted to let her know that Eric and I are trying to work it out and I was just with him. It was December 13th, the day I was going over to see the Trans-Siberian Orchestra for my Christmas gift to myself and she finally replied nastily to me. She was so mean and said that her and "Eric are still friends and I talk to him every day and night and I want him for myself. I don't care if you were with him yesterday. He is mine. I trust him, not you. Leave me alone."

It threw me for a loop and I was sobbing crying and I didn't understand why she was so mean to me. I was just trying to reach out and be nice, but she was very mad to hear that we were talking again. I messaged and called Eric to tell him and ask him why? And he didn't know what to say other than, "Why are you messaging her anyways? You guys aren't friends," and I said, "Maybe we don't need to be friends, but we don't need to be enemies." He made us enemies by whatever he told her. I'm sure he made nice with her again and keeps her around for the benefits.

During this time, since I wasn't being treated how I wanted to be, I went out for a coffee date with a Facebook friend who asked me out for coffee. I said okay. I met up with him and we just had coffee and breakfast. I ended up telling Eric and he lost his mind. Treated me like I was the worst person in the world. Called me all sorts of names. Slut and a whore. He got so mad. Just because I went out for breakfast. There was no kiss, no nothing. But he lost his mind. I told him nothing has been the same and he wasn't treating me like he used to, so if I'm going to still be single, I'm going to act like it. He didn't like that at all.

I ended it with Eric and I actually ended up going out on a couple dates with this particular man. We ended up coming back to my place and I ended up "with" him and I ended up crying in the middle of it. I felt terrible. The first man I was with after Eric. Apparently, I was not ready to be with someone else. I only add this in here, to show how someone can "be with" another person without any emotions whatsoever and another person, can't even do that even when everything is over. I just couldn't do it. I felt like I was cheating on him and I wasn't…he was. Always was. And I don't know how someone can do that with no emotional response. It was awful and I felt terrible.

February/March 2020; Then COVID hit

When COVID hit, I reached out to him. I wanted to make sure him and his dad were okay. I know I'm a glutton for punishment…but I have a heart and I wanted to know they were okay. Especially his dad. I've always liked his dad, and I wanted to make sure everyone was okay.

Of course, that started some communication and always a night with him…and always ended with questions….

Until I finally reached out to one of his neighbors in the community in April….Finally.

Master of deceit, King of lies

Even today, over a year after I found out, I still miss him and I don't know why. I know what he did is unforgivable to take him back. I go to church, and I have my church family and all of my friends, family, and kids.

I'm fine without him…I just keep telling myself that.

After I found out he was actually seeing someone since October (or before I believe, I believe she's the same girl from the very beginning, since January) and I left him a message to tell him I know and to leave me alone. I was not polite at all. My message went something like this, "So I found out you've been seeing someone else for MONTHS now! I WILL find out who she is and I will expose you for the lying, cheating, narcissistic, sociopath piece of shit that you are. God's wrath is coming after you. All those wasted prayers on you, hoping you could change, but I was wrong."

Granted, I won't look for her and tell her, however I will pray for her that her eyes will be opened and she will SEE for herself what kind of man she's with. It's only a matter of time. This man can't and won't be faithful. EVER.

I had him blocked, so he showed up at my door the next morning while I was on the phone with my friend Tami. He always does that. He loves the chase, plus he wanted to find out where I was getting my information and wanted to see how much I knew, I'm sure.

He had the audacity to act like it wasn't true, with a little smirk on his face that I wanted to smack off of him, he said to me, "Wherever you're getting your information from it isn't true."

But I knew it was true; my sources are very, very reliable and I believe this person over him any day.

I even videotaped him a little bit out front, begging me to believe him.

Long story short, since I was not caving in to him. He came clean and last I've heard he was going to "break up" with her and try and get back together with me. Kept saying it has always been you. I've always wanted you.

I call bullshit.

I won't ever take him back and I don't believe that he'll break up with her. He'll make up some grand scheme to try and get me back and keep her…

And that is exactly what he did.

Two weeks later, he called me saying that he did it, he broke up with her. I taped the phone recording this time. I got smart so if she ever reached out to me, I have evidence of him trying to get back together with me.

I reached out to my acquaintance to see if she was still at his house and sure enough, she was there that night.

It's always the same story: "He didn't know how to get rid of them without hurting their feelings." In this case, her. Instead, he tore me apart. Every. Time.

He said he didn't want to end it with her if I was going to leave again. However, I told him I wanted to start all over in December, July…that I really wanted to try again. But he was with her, was with her the whole time we were seeing each other then and in February and now, just a couple of days ago. It sickens me, but I'm so extremely glad I've found out the truth. That I know and am friends with one of his neighbors that could confirm what I was thinking but had no proof.

I finally was able to expose him for the lying, cheating, deceitful man that he is.

A devil in disguise.

I don't believe for one second any longer, that he loves me or ever loved me at all! After all this, this man is incapable of love and is full of lies.

Master of deceit and the King of lies.

I'm *soooo* happy and glad I see through all of the bullshit now. It took way too long and now I have to figure out what is wrong with ME to have gone through all this, for way too long. To go back and forth with him over and over? What is wrong with me?

I need to find my self-worth, self-love, and self-confidence.

That is what I'll be working on for a while…

I need to work on forgiveness towards him and myself for allowing this to go on for too long.

This is my promise to myself from this day forward.

Wishing I had never looked back

Realizing Eric has actually been seeing someone for what I believe to be a whole year, all the while, trying to get me back and us going back and forth, has got me thinking…

How could I be so stupid? I'm such an idiot! Of course, he's been with someone else this whole time! I'm no one special, not like he made me feel I was. If he could be with two other women the whole time I was with him, how could he not have been with someone new this whole time? Hello! Another girl. I'm certain, if she basically lives with him, they have been together probably since that January. I started getting suspicious. If she was doing work around the yard and sweeping the driveway like I was told, she had already moved in and lives with him. That tears me apart.

Since Jill and Kathy are gone, he had to fill up his time with another girl. Which in reality, makes me feel not good enough and unworthy. I was the "other girl" now. I mean, why was I not good enough to be his "only" girl? What was wrong with me? He knew I wanted all of his time, yet he kept choosing to give part of himself to someone else…the WHOLE time I was with him, he was never really "with" me. He was never really mine.

I guess I never really wanted to see or accept the reality of it all.

Now he had been cheating on her with me. Before he was cheating on me with her, how the tables have turned. And now he comes knocking on my door telling me he'd leave her to be with me? Oh, hell no! He'd just find a way to keep her and let me back in. I don't need him, nor want him any longer. I don't believe him for a second. And not only that, I'd never trust him ever again. He can't be with just one girl, he can't be faithful, and he can't be trusted.

I started counseling a couple weeks ago and I had a lot of revelations. In the last session we uncovered that I'm afraid that I'll never find what I thought I had with Eric, that I'll never find the love of my life and I'll never feel that way again. That's why I kept trying. I kept trying to get back what I "felt." Sometimes I miss him so much, especially writing all the good things about him and all the great memories we made just being together and traveling.

I have to remember what kind of man he really is. This man will never change, not without deep healing counseling that would last for at least a year. Do I miss him, yes and no. Do I love him…not anymore. Thank God.

I miss the person I was with him.

He made me feel good.

He made me be good.

He made me feel on top of the world.

Until the fairy-tale world got ripped out from under my feet.

If I just didn't call that psychic in November, I wouldn't have even reached back out to him again. I wouldn't have had that hope that we could actually make it work again. There was always that glimmer of hope that made me keep coming back to try. If I could get back what we had, it would be worth it.

But oh, how I was wrong and oh how I wish I had never done that; I'd be so much better by now. Now that I'm getting counseling for myself and wondering what the hell is wrong with me!

Should have never had hope, should have never loved him so much. That hope is deep down in the deepest part of the ocean's bottom, locked in a box and it's never coming back up.

My good friend Susan said this to me once and it has stuck in my head ever since and no truer words than these:

"There comes a time you need to love yourself more,"

And that time is right now.

I choose me. Always and Forever.

Do I make mistakes and have moments of weakness, yes, but I am only human, in a messy, hard and hurtful situation.

It will take time and that's okay.

I LOVE ME MORE! From this day forward. I love me more!

He Moved On—All those wasted prayers on him

He has been with someone else for months, maybe even a year. I was just some side fling he could take advantage of once in a while. He probably enjoyed that I was still hanging on to him for a year and not moved on. I had been with him off and on for a year. I only wish I knew then what I know now.

Although I did know, I just didn't want to listen to myself and I only have myself to blame, thinking that someone like that could change, thinking I was enough that he would change, its heartbreaking. All those wasted prayers on him. On a man who cannot and will not be faithful.

I was always told, "just pray for him," and I did for a while. I prayed that whatever evil force had its grip on him would let him go. I prayed that his heart to be healed and he would be happy, whole, and healed.

I came to realize that me praying for him kept me connected to him, which kept me thinking and wishing he would change and come around. I was wrong….

A tiger doesn't change his stripes.

All the weekends he wouldn't spend with me, saying he was with friends doing stuff. I would say, let's start over, but he would never show up for me like he used to. I guess I wasn't as special as he once made me feel.

All along he was with his new girl.

He claimed he hadn't been with anyone and claimed to only be on a couple of dates, nothing serious. Although at the very mention of me going on a breakfast day with someone, he lost his mind, started screaming at me, calling me a slut and a whore. And when I said, I had been with two people while we were broken up, he freaked out on me screaming at me, saying, "How could you do this to me? Someday someone is going to hurt you and do the same thing you did to me."

Wow, just wow! And What the Fuck?! Really! Didn't you just cheat on me with two other women…now a third…three that I know of…if the whole truth ever came out, it probably be a whole lot more.

I can't tell you how many times, we were on the phone, and he'd be screaming at me so bad, I would put the phone down and I could still hear him clearly. He was awful. Terrible person.

Now I realize he has been with someone else this whole time.

But that's what narcissists do.

They turn everything around on you and make you look and feel like you're the bad one.

I'm just so glad I found out and can finally move on to find someone I deserve and who deserves me…someday.

But I realize I need some help and counseling. After a year and I still want to go back to this man is awful. I should have moved on right away and not allowed him access to my heart after that horrible truth about him came out. Sometimes I wish I didn't have such a hopeful heart. Thought praying for him every day would change him. But that man will never change and even if he did, he will never deserve me again.

I AM DONE!

Chapter 3
Healed

Healing:
    They say the passage of time will heal all wounds,
    But the greater the loss the deeper the cut.
    Thus, the more difficult the process to become whole again.
    The pain may fade but the scars serve as a reminder
    and makes the barrier to never be wounded again.
    So as the time moves along, we get lost in distractions,
    act out in frustration, react in aggression, and give in to anger.
    All the while we plot and plan a way to grow stronger,
    and before we know it, the time passes,
    we are healed and ready to begin anew.

                                      -Klaus Mikaelson

After having a hard him moving on and wondering why I couldn't, I decided to start doing all the things he did for me, but I'll do them for myself. That is when I started traveling. Taking myself out to dinner and doing all the things he did, but for myself.

    I planned on doing a six months to a year Self-Love journey. What I came to realize, this journey that I began that November 1st, 2019, was a journey that I'll be doing for the rest of my life. I've become happier, stronger, self-reliant, and self-sufficient. This is the first time in my whole entire life that I am happy being me. Happy with my life.

This is my story. This is my "Healing" journey.

This is the first time in my existence that I've taken the time to heal on my own, not dating period, and actually learning to love myself the way I need to be loved. Recognizing my worth.

Some of it is not pretty and it's pretty messy. But healing isn't always supposed to be pretty. It takes work and it gets lonely. It's hard, but it's worth it and the greatest thing I've done for myself.

I am happy.

I am content.

I love myself.

I love my life.

I have built a life that I love and I'm excited about.

And you can too.

Journey to Self

I'll take care of myself. I don't need anyone. I am really good alone.

Would I want someone in my future? Yes, but I have to realize that I won't get what I had back and that's okay. And I don't even want that back. I'm looking for something different, something better. I'm a hopeless romantic at heart. I know eventually I'll find someone and feel something again. It's just going to take time. Time is all I need. For now, I'm happy on my own. Working on me first.

I have learned a lot from my past. I am smarter now. I may have trust issues, even with myself and I have a lot to work on by myself. But I can say I'm actually happy where I am at this time in my life.

A journey to Self:

Self-Love

Self-Worth

Self-Acceptance

Self-Discovery

Self-Confidence

Praying
It's 3 am.
You'd think I'd be over him,
But I still wake up thinking about him.
Nightmares and bad dreams,
Tossing, turning, and thinking
About what he did to me.
Wishing,
Hoping and praying.
It'll all just go away.
Every day gets better,
Every day closer to forgetting,
Now that the pain is lessening.
Praying,
God, please take this away.
Praying,
God, please do the vengeance.
Praying,
God, please help me to forgive.
I cannot do this on my own,
I need your help,
To heal, to forgive, and help me get back up again.

Face to Face with your own Demons
How can you trust someone?
When you don't even trust yourself.
When my walls are up and
I won't let my guard come down.
You will have to slowly crawl
Towards me so that I will not run.

You will have to climb these walls
Just to come near to me.
I'm good where I am.
In between these walls I've made.
Protected and safe,
It's only me I have to see...

Being my own hero
I was raped, but you hurt me more.
I was married and divorced, but you hurt me more.
I was engaged and broken, but YOU hurt me more.
I wanted you more than anything,
I loved you more than I've ever loved anyone.
But you tore me apart;
With all your lies and betrayal.
I gave you more chances than anyone deserved.
And you still couldn't or wouldn't show up for me.
Still pursuing and playing your games.
I didn't betray you; I didn't hurt you; I didn't abandon you.
YOU DID.
All your lies and all your girls.
You made me feel worthless and undeserving.
I'm loving myself and being my own hero.
Loving myself the way you did but better.
Loyal, faithful with an unconditional love and respect.
I deserve way better than you.
And, you...
You never deserved me.

Don't wait till your heart is torn apart
When you want someone to love you so much,
And when you love someone so much,

You want to overlook the signs that are right there in front of you…
Don't wait till your heart is torn apart and shattered.
When you see the first sign of red flags, go. Walk away.
People don't change.
There is no amount of crying, pleading, wishing, or praying that will get him to change.
Don't waste another year like I did, hoping like I did.
I believe in hope, but you need to hope for and love yourself more
And hope for a better future without him.
Someday it'll get better and the pain will lessen;
Not with time, they say, but with intention,
With self-healing.
You have to do the work.
You have to Love YOU!
You deserve it and you deserve happiness.

Self-Love
You stole my heart;
I asked you to protect it,
But you didn't just break it,
You crushed it.
Now I'm busy picking up
The pieces.
Meshing and lovingly binding them back together.
I vow never to allow someone
The access to hurt me like that again.
Now it's time to love myself
The way you did, but didn't.
I'll never let myself down,
Never betray and lie.
I'll protect and guard my heart.
Love myself like no one else can.

Never going back to you
A year ago, you broke my heart, the truth came out and I fell apart.
But now I
Thank you….
Thank you for turning me into the
Strongest womsn I've ever been
Thank you for making me turn in and look up.
Because of you, now I know what I'm worth and what I deserve.
And now I can say I love myself more than I ever loved you.
And I'm never going back to you
And what you put me through.

Memories
Here comes all the memories…
This mind full of memories
I don't want to remember.
I just want this hell to be over.
Not sleeping because it plays over and over in my head, wondering why?
Why I couldn't see it?
Wishing I wasn't all true.
Wishing it really was just a nightmare and I'd wake up to.
My dreams came crashing down in New York
That December Sunday Morning.
I wish my fairytale didn't end up being the nightmare I can't get out of.

Why?
Why do some men or women date multiple people?

    Why do some women fear commitment so much that they only date married men?

    Why do some people, no matter what, keep going back into the same type of toxic, abusive, or failing relationships?

Because most of us don't take the necessary time it takes to heal. We walk around thinking everything is okay, we mask the pain by replacing it with the newest attraction we can find (whether that's drugs, alcohol, sex, or a brand-new relationship).

Yet we don't take the time to look deep inside and patch up our wounds the healthy way and instead, we look to others to do what we should be doing ourselves and get upset at the person for failing to do what only God can do (heal our brokenness).

Then we are left with yet another failed relationship, more bitter, more hurt and more wounded. Do you know what hurt people do? They hurt people. Hence, the cycle begins or continues and now we have a bunch of hurt people walking around hurting people. No wonder we are living in a fallen world. Wounded people walking.

What if we ALL took the time to heal our inner wounds?

What a wonderful world it would be.

We are all broken. We all have been through messy, dirty, ugly, horrible, human stuff. We all have been hurt, yet we've all hurt people too. We've all done some bad things. At some point this cycle has to stop.

We all deserve redemption. We all deserve forgiveness. We all deserve to be loved and accepted.

But first and foremost, we all need to heal.

We deserve to heal our inner wounds so we can BE healthy, be IN a healthy relationship with not only someone else but more importantly, yourself.

Learn to love yourself and learn to love being BY yourself. The way to do that is to draw closer to God and He will draw closer to you. Then you're never really alone.

Healing...

Healing is staying home, yet going out with friends.

It's reading books, yet binge watching your favorite shows.

It's reading daily devotionals and crying until you can't anymore.

It's refusing to contact him when you start to miss him…again.

It's telling yourself over and over it wasn't you and you're worth so much more.

It's feeling the pain, sitting with the loneliness, and making it through just one more day…

I'll put these pieces back together like never before and I'll be better than ever before.

With Intention

It took a long time to put those pieces back together…I'm so glad to be here…happy and healed.

I know all too well how it feels to not be able to get out of bed. To feel pain that cuts so deep you wonder how you're ever going to survive. You may feel lost or may feel as if you won't be able to make it. But time does heal all wounds and I can tell you now, you will feel better again. Not just with time, but with intention. It's what you DO in that time that matters the most. Find yourself and find yourself good friends to help you get through the darkness.

When you get on the other side of this pain, you will be a beacon of light for others going through what you are going through now. Be patient and don't give up. There is light in the darkness you're going through.

I will Survive!

Depression is a killer, a killer of dreams, a killer of hope.
It makes you want to want to stay in bed all morning and cry.
One day you think you're doing better and begin to see the light,
the next it makes you feel like your life is over.
Depression says you're weak and worthless.
It's the feeling of being alone, and no one cares.
Depression is a liar.
Depression is not your friend.
Depression is evil seeping in to bring you down.
But I'm stronger than my depression.
And I will survive!

I find my hope in God.
God is my friend.
God will break these chains.
And I will see the light again.

Who you are is up to you…don't leave it up to them.

To have big dreams you must start somewhere, you have to at least try.

You do not know what you can do unless you step out of your comfort zone and just do it!

You'll be surprised at what you can do and how far you can go.

I used to try and figure out how to make more money so I could pay bills and survive. Now I figure out how to make more money so I can play and THRIVE!

Goal-setting is such an important tool to reach your dreams, and to turn those dreams into reality!

Anything that you desire and want CAN be achieved…first you need to believe it can be done and then begin on the steps you need to DO to bring your dream to reality!

Growth
You may not like me
But that's okay,
I love me.
It took me a long time to even like myself,
So your opinion of me
Doesn't matter at all.
You may have heard of me,
But you don't know me.
You may know me,
But you don't know my story.
I've worked hard to get to where I am today.
Felt pain and disappointment,
Most people wouldn't be able to handle.

But I made it and
I'm proud of myself.
And
If you knew my story,
You'd be proud too.

Grow Church

The start of my healing process started with the twenty-one days of prayer in August 2019 at Grow Church. I had started going there right before Eric and I broke it off. He had even been there with me a few times.

I was not doing well at all and decided to join a home-based prayer group. Every night they had a meeting at 7:00 p.m. at a home, I attended at Paster Mary's. Every morning they had a meeting at 6:00 a.m. at the church. I tried to make it to at least one a day. It was really hard, but I desperately needed the help, support, and prayers. It was very nice when they all would pray over me. I believe this church and church members were really there to help me get through what I was battling…the enemy…evil.

From there I joined a Freedom group, which changed my life. It was a women's freedom group to break the chains of the past, something I desperately needed. There were chapters on worthiness and forgiveness. The group of women I met through this group was amazing and now I have built lasting friendships with them. There were times I broke down, crying hysterically, almost hyperventilating. These women helped build me up and put me back together again.

From there I was baptized in November, I took the classes to become a member, and started volunteering and then got baptized!

Presently I've been tithing, and I recently just wrote this testimony:
8/10/20

"I started tithing before COVID began and kept tithing throughout COVID. During this time, I've made a lot of changes to my business. I raised my prices in the middle of this and my life has been blossoming in all areas of my life. I had to get my car fixed and still went on vacation with no worry.

Anytime a worry comes up, I know God will take care of me as I'm taking of his children. I pray every day, state my needs, and pray He sends me the clients and customers who need me. I pray the power of protection and healing over myself, my family, friends, and clients. Prayer and tithing are something I love to do, and I do it with enthusiasm and joy. It's not a burden when it's life-changing and empowering. God Is Good…all the time.

The way I see it, if God can pull me out of the rut and the severe depression I was in, from wanting to kill myself to living an amazing and fulfilling life, finding joy again and blesses me with abundance of every kind, the least I can do is give a tithe back to Him and his Kingdom. Because truly if I didn't have Him, Grow Church, and its amazing members, all of my amazing friends and of course the big reason, my kids, I'm not sure I would have made it out alive.

People, we need people, we need community. We need our Tribe. Go find your Tribe and Survive!

November 2019/Self Love Month

November 1st. I looked at my closet and thought, "That's it! I'm getting rid of that dress!" The wedding dress I had kept in my closet for two years now. The dress I was supposed to wear for Dave, my ex-fiancé. We were supposed to be marred November 11th, 2017. That's another awful story.

I got up and said, "I'm going to get rid of EVERYTHING I don't need anymore, so I took my $1,100 wedding dress and many other things and dropped them off to Goodwill. I did a deep cleaning, cleansing, and purging of my place. Took pictures I had of Eric and me, ripped and threw them away. Cleaned everything, then saged to get all of the bad energy out of my house. Boy was my place full of sage! Whatever demons or evil, bad energy that was there had no way of surviving! I choked them OUT OF MY LIFE!

Then I put up my Christmas Tree.

I LOVE Christmas and it makes me happy. Right now everything is about me, not in a conceited way, but in a healthy, "I've never done this before," Self-love way.

Then I decided, why don't I make this a self-love month?

Which lasted into the year and into the next…and will NEVER stop!

I began by cleaning out the old, so I could bring in the new.

I took the classes to join my church, got baptized, and joined the freedom group (to break the chains of the past). Went to the Saturday night sunset worship at the beach and had dinner with a new girlfriend from that night.

I let myself feel. I didn't try and mask the pain. I went through all the emotions. It wasn't pretty, but it was good and very much needed.

I bought myself flowers, I got my hair cut short, had a pedicure with a glass of wine. I ate well. I rested.

I felt.

My Trip to Asheville; November 17, 2019

I went to Asheville by myself. The first time I went anywhere alone. I had a great time. I went to the Biltmore Estates for their Christmas event. It was an amazing, beautiful place with Christmas trees everywhere. For a girl who loves Christmas, I was in Christmas heaven!

After taking the tour of the house, I went to the winery…of course, I had to go there! As I was standing there, waiting to be seated, another single lady came and stood by me. We ended up getting sat together. It was really nice.

She was from the Northeast. We never talked about why both of us traveled alone to Ashville. I just know she had her own story…but for the evening, we were just two single ladies just trying to find their way by getting lost.

The first morning I was there, I got up early and wanted to watch the sunrise over the mountains. I went down to the lobby and the receptionist looked at me like I was crazy, he said, "You know there's a blizzard outside, right? It's raining out right now and even the school buses are delayed."

I replied, "No, I just got in from Florida yesterday, I had no idea there was bad weather coming!"

So, I sat by the fireplace in the dining room area and ate breakfast. It was very lovely.

The next couple days, I explored the downtown area, walked around everywhere. It was pretty cool.

It was so cold when I went there. It was the first cold spell Asheville had and it was freezing for me—40 degrees! Every coffee shop I saw, I stopped in and had a mocha, to keep me warm. My favorite was the Champagne bar and bookstore, other than the Biltmore Christmas estate. You could get a glass of champagne, a cheese plate and browse the old used bookstore. It was so cool.

My last day there, my friend, Alex, who lived up there, picked me up and we went to a nature area and went out to dinner and then he did a healing on me and helped me talk through my problems. I journaled and did self-healing and then flew back home the next day.

My only regret of the trip was not renting a car so I could go into the mountains. Whenever I travel again, I will definitely get a rental car! First trip, lesson learned!

All in all, it was a great trip.

Thanksgiving 2019

This Thanksgiving had been a good one, it is like a switch got flipped and I'm finally feeling better. I went up to Sarasota to be with my good friend Christine and her family. It was a great day. The kids and I took turns saying something that we were grateful for on the ride up there. It is so nice to concentrate on what you're grateful for. It really turns your focus around on what you don't want to what you do want and what you want more of.

If you incorporate "giving thanks" into your daily routine, I guarantee you will see your life change little by little. I keep a gratefulness jar on my kitchen counter so the kids and I can write what we are grateful for during the year and around New Year's we sit around the dinner table and read them. It has become a great family-time practice. The more grateful you are, the more present you become, the more joy you bring into your life.

I had been in a depressed state for at least week, after I got back from Asheville. I was constantly replaying everything in my mind. It was like being in hell.

The more I thought about everything the more depressed I got. Thinking that the next two months are going to be horrible. But I finally broke away from that. I started saying, "My mind is free, clear, and happy" over and over. Eventually the depression I was feeling for the last week lifted and I made the best out of the next two months. He would not ruin the holidays for me. Nope, I would not allow him that power over me.

If you turn your thoughts around, your life will begin to get better. Sometimes we are held captive; not by someone else or by what they did, but by our own mind. Once I started to think about all that I do have, all that I'm thankful for and focusing on my future and what I have planned for myself and my kids, I started to become happier.

He has taken enough from me; he doesn't deserve any more. I was able to see Christmas in New York and see the Christmas tree, #1 on my bucket list. He's not going to take that memory away from me. My 40th birthday party he threw for me. All great memories and I'm thankful for every single one of them. He can't take that from me.

December 2019

In December I was really worried that I'd have a horrible month after everything that happened the year before, going to New York with him and having such a magical time…and then finding out about the other girl. But I was determined to have an amazing month. I love Christmas and I would NOT let him take that away from me!

At the beginning of the month, December 8th, after the Freedom conference, I took myself out on a date for a dinner and a show. I bought myself a beautiful new dress; it was dark red, short, sparkly, and was form-fitting at the top then opened up at the bottom. It was so cute! And I looked good! Dressed up and out all by myself!

I had always wanted to go to see a Cirque Show so I got myself tickets to see a "Magical Christmas" Cirque Show for my Christmas present for myself and went to Roy's Restaurant. I had never been there before and had always wanted to check it out.

First, I went to the restaurant. I sat at the bar, which made me feel a little bit awkward at first. There was a man sitting next to me and two women sitting on the other side of me. I had a good conversation with all of them and I had a conversation with the gentleman next to me about what success really is. He was talking about how his daughter works in a nature center and doesn't make a lot of money. Which I'm sure he did, after working in the financial industry in downtown Manhattan. I had told him that, "success isn't about how much money you make, but about how happy you are and even if you have a lot of money, that doesn't guarantee that will make you happy. The main goal in life is to be happy." He replied, "I like your outlook on life. It's refreshing."

It is ironic however that I meet someone from Manhattan, who worked in the financial industry, while I'm on my healing journey and date night while getting over my ex who was from that area and worked in the financial industry also. I feel that some things happen, to test you, but also to help you find your strength. It is not to defeat you, but to help you. You can overcome and you can heal. It didn't trigger me. It helped me.

Then I went to the show. I went up and got myself a glass of wine and asked a couple people to take some pictures of me in front of the Christmas theme show backdrops. I had so many people come up to me and compliment me on my dress and shoes. I was standing by the door to the entrance, waiting for the doors to open to the show and a gentleman walked up to me and asked me if I had good tickets, I said no because I had bought my tickets late and I had last row tickets. He said, "I have an extra ticket right up front; do you want it?" I said, "Heck yes, I do!" I ended up sitting front row, middle!

Great seats, at a great show. I was in awe and I felt so lucky to be single and to have that opportunity! Sometimes good things happen when you're single. The gentleman was just a nice guy, his wife was just sick and couldn't make it. He never tried to hit on me. It was just a nice evening. I truly enjoyed myself.

Then, on December 13th, I took myself to see the Trans-Siberian Orchestra for my birthday present to myself. Another thing I've always wanted to do but hadn't. The Trans-Siberian Orchestra plays my favorite Christmas song.

I drove to the East Coast; it was in Sunrise, Florida. I got myself some wine and went to go sit in the suite that I got for myself. I was one of the first people there, so I got to pick my seats. I sat right in the corner, closest to the stage.

It was such an amazing show. I was in such awe. I would definitely do that again a thousand times over! Highly recommend!

Since I sat where I did, there was only one seat right beside me. I think a lot of people were mad at me for taking a spot with only two seats; someone even came up to me and said something, but I told her as well as the couple behind me said we can sit anywhere, we don't have assigned seats. It's a first-come-first-serve basis. Even the couple behind me was like, you were here first. I kind of felt bad, but this was all about me, and I was putting myself first for once in my life. I'm pretty sure I was probably the only single person there. I am fine with that. It is very powerful and freeing to go and do anything that you want with or without someone.

Later that month, on my birthday, December 22nd, I took my boys up to St. Pete to the Enchant Christmas Maze! I was so super excited to see this! It travels around and only comes down to Florida every once in a while! It was pretty cool. We got hot cocoa and walked around the huge Christmas lighted sculptures. We stayed on the beach on St. Pete for two days. It was a pretty cool place; it had a tiki bar and a restaurant and game area the boys liked to play at and we walked down the beach area and went to the tiki bar for dinner and listened to the band. It was a great time. I met some new friends there, a very nice couple. I even became friends with the lady on Facebook. I really liked her.

From there we went up to Orlando to go to Disney for the boys' first time. My son had wanted to go pretty bad and we hadn't gone yet. I like to do things with them for Christmas. To me, making memories is the best thing you can do! So, Christmas Eve we went, which was a mistake! It was so crowded, but we still made it a great time. We watched the parade and went to the hotel and came back later for the evening and watched the Christmas show. That was a nice part. It was just so crowded you could barely walk anywhere and the rides were too long to wait.

We stayed at the Disney's Sports Hotel, which was the coolest hotel I'd ever been in. I had a great time with my boys. Always have a good time with them.

Charleston for Valentine's Day

Valentine's Day 2020, I went to Charleston by myself, the very first Valentine's Day I've had alone. It was the best experience. I had such a great time! I arrived in the late evening on Friday (Valentine's Day) got my rental car, and went straight to my Airbnb that I got in Summerville. It was a cute little studio room above a garage. I just loved it; it was perfect just for me. It was filled with blue tones, had a small kitchenette, a cute little table, and chairs with some fake flowers. I was staying here for two nights. I went to bed, and when I got up, I got ready, and went to the local coffee shop there, before I went to John's Island where I went to the Tea Plantation, the Angel Oak Tree, and the Winery.

The local coffee shop I went to was in their downtown area. A very small place, I walked down the main street and noticed a place I'd like to come back to that evening, called Accent on Wine. Right up my alley!

I started out to St. John Island; the hour drive alone was so beautiful! I went to the Angel Tree first. It was a 400-year-old oak tree. It was amazing. For my souvenirs, I picked up a post card at each place I went. Then I went to the winery. I loved that place, my favorite part of the trip. I tasted the wines and had a glass of wine and cheese and sat outside. They had a lot of land and it was beautiful just sitting out there. From there I went to the tea plantation. I learned that the tea plantation is the only tea manufacturer in the United States, that grows AND harvests it. I took a tour of how they produce and make their teas. I saw a bench with a statue of a frog on it, so I took a selfie with him and posted it on Facebook saying, "I found my prince, he's been at the tea plantation this whole time!"

From there I went back to the winery for food and music and just hung out there for an hour and headed back into Summerville. My hostess at the Airbnb has a coffee shop so I went there for a coffee and to say hi. It was really good coffee and a super cute place. Like a coffee and wine bar. I sat at the bar area, enjoying my coffee and the scenery. From there I went back to my place and got ready to go out to eat at the Accent on Wine. I got all dressed up in my pretty pink dress. When I arrived at the restaurant, I went up to the bar area and ordered a glass of wine and a cheese plate. It was very good. I enjoyed the wine, food, atmosphere, and the people. From there I went back to my place for the night.

The next morning was a Sunday. I got up early and headed into Charleston so I could go to church. I found a parking spot for $10 for six hours, which I thought was pretty good and perfect timing until I checked into my bed in breakfast I was staying at that night. I wanted to go into one of the oldest churches and attend their service. I went to a Unitarian Church built in 1787. It was a really nice service; nice people and they had an after-church social that I went to. After that, I went to Queen 82 and had some She Crab soup everyone told me to try and a mimosa for lunch.

Then, I walked around and waited until my room at John Rutledge House was ready. I went to "The Market"—the story behind it was really sad. They sell handmade keepsakes and lots of other items. It is a pretty neat place!

I went back to the John Rutledge house, the historic mansion I was staying at for the night. I paid a pretty penny to stay here, but it was so worth it. For my first Valentine's Day by myself, I am going to treat myself like a queen and that's how I felt staying there. My room ready, so I moved my car and checked in. I had ordered myself a cheese tray to be in the room when I got there. I wanted to buy myself a bottle of champagne, but the receptionist said it would be best if I walked to the grocery and get a bottle there. So, as they were getting my cheese ready, I walked to the store and on my way back, I went into a chocolate shop and got myself some heart-shaped champagne chocolates and some chocolate macaroons.

I came back to my room and my cheese board was there. It was amazing! So many different cheeses, meats, nuts, jams, and crackers. What a tray! As I sat there alone, in my room, eating cheese and drinking my champagne, it was the first time I felt alone and sad. I kept telling myself, this is good for me. So, I just sat in my loneliness, and drank my champagne. Sat with my feelings, thought…and healed. Healing is not easy, or fun. But you have to work through the pain, the loneliness, the anger if you ever want to be better than ever before.

At 8:00 p.m., I signed up for a ghost and beer tour, called the Boo-Hag and Brews Tour. That was a lot of fun, with a good group of people. We walked around all the spooky churches and graveyards, while he told us all the cool, spooky stories.

The next morning, I woke up and walked to Rainbow Row and down by the water's edge. The Rainbow Row was so cool and walking down by the water was so refreshing, and I was so happy right there in that moment, smiling ear to ear. This is what healing is all about. Being completely happy all by yourself, taking in all the scenery, loving every minute, even the uncomfortable ones. Because those minutes will be the ones that bring you the most happiness, success, and pride in the future. This is what love is and I'm showing and giving it all to myself. What a great and amazing thing! To finally love myself the way I always should have been. I am worth it!

Something to be proud of

I had a rough morning; I was going through my journal to see if there was anything in there good enough to add into my book. Having to go through all the good and the bad, and then going through this book to look through it and touch it up a bit, I just started crying. I've kind of pushed everything down and away, since I found out he had been with someone else the whole time (the third girl). I didn't even want to feel it anymore. I feel angry and stupid all at the same time. So, the last few months, even though I've been going to counseling and still doing my self-care, I've been drinking entirely way to much plus with this COVID-19 thing going on, it's just been a little rough.

So, I've been on a no-alcohol kick for five days now, and since I was having such a tough day, I really wanted a drink…really, really, really bad.

I even had my neighbor come down to help me zip up my new dress, and she comes down with a glass of wine. I could have easily asked her for some, but I didn't. Some of my friends said, just go get a small bottle of wine and have one glass…but I didn't. I didn't even get into my vodka I have in the freezer.

Instead, I came home from work, got myself some beautiful roses and carnation bouquet, my friend came over and gave me a massage, and then I had my counseling appointment (which is going so good, getting into and healing my childhood trauma) then did my workout. Continued reading my journal to pick out worthy entries, freaked out a little bit more, talked to some friends, then took my self-love bath and drank my stress reliever infused water.

I'm feeling pretty proud of myself for not caving and reaching for the alcohol!

I will pat myself on the back. I LOVE ME MORE!

Self-Love

For the last several months, my Thursdays have consisted of buying myself flowers, getting counseling, and then ending the evening with what I call a "Love me Bath," where I do a detox bath with Epsom salts, baking soda, essential oils, bubble bath, and rose petals. Surrounded with candles and a glass of wine. Then I take markers and write all over myself about how much I love myself and write the words from the Ho'oponopono prayer, which are: *I love you, I'm sorry, Please forgive me, Thank you.*

It is a powerful prayer I say to myself everyday all day long and towards others.

Then I use a salt scrub and also say out loud the Ho'oponopono prayer while massaging myself and then I lay back and relax and read one of my self-love books. I'm reading all the codependent books I can find at the moment.

About the Ho'oponopono prayer and my morning ritual:

Every morning when I wake up, I start with prayer. On my dresser I have my altar where I light my incense and I say the Ho'oponopono over and over as I look at some pictures of my younger self for self-healing, I say a clearing prayer while I light some sage to get rid of any negativity and then I say the Lord's prayer. I pray for my needs, in "Thank you God for" sentences as if I've already achieved what I desire and then I state my needs, wants, and desires and I let it go to God/Spirit. I then go over the seventy-two names of God and pray for others. I meditate, visualize, write my affirmations, read, journal and exercise. It is a great way to start your day motivated and focused. Eyes on your goals. Energized and happy.

The Ho'oponopono is an ancient Hawaiian practice and is well-known for clearing negativity from one's mind and thoughts. Dr. Joe Vital says, "It is believed to be designed to wipe out all the negativity in our thoughts and those blocks that are keeping us miserable. There is a large number of us who don't have the luxury of enjoying peace. This practice is designed to remove all the stress and negativity from your mind. It is a simple technique where you ask for forgiveness and purifying yourself and by doing that, you not only help yourself but you help others as well. Do yourself a favor and do some research of this, you will be happy you did. 'I love you, I'm sorry, Please forgive me, Thank you.'"

Fast forward to a couple months, now I'm actually starting to date a little. I'm feeling much better, happier, and healthier. I'm shining! My life is amazing! I'm at the best I've ever been and I'm so proud of myself! I'm not ready to throw myself into a full-blown relationship yet, but I'm ready to get my feet wet a little bit. But more importantly, still work on me.

Now I'll be smarter and be able to see the red flags or see what it is that "I" want.

I know now what is important to me.

And what is not.

I'm more important. My needs are important.

This is my life and now since I'm at a place I don't need someone.

I'm not even sure I want someone anymore…which is such a freeing feeling.

Being happy alone.

Do the healing you need.

It will be the best work you'll ever do for yourself and your future self will thank you…

As well as the future person you bring into your life. But make sure your future person you bring into your life is where you are, and has done the work you have, you don't want to go backwards, you want to keep growing.

It may be uncomfortable, and you may feel like you can't, but you can. If I can, you definitely can. Get through those feelings and emotions. Treat yourself the way you want to be treated. There is no reason to have to wait for someone else to do for you what you want. Go do it yourself! Love yourself the way you want to be loved! So, when someone comes into your life, they'll be a bonus, not your all and everything. Plus, you are giving them a handbook on how you want to be treated.

Do it for yourself.

You want flowers. Buy yourself flowers.

You want to go out to eat? Take yourself out to dinner. Dress up. Love yourself!

You want to travel? Go somewhere you've always wanted to go.

You want to have a ring? Buy yourself one!

Everything you want a man to do for you, do for yourself.

I assure you, you will feel so much more empowered by giving to yourself.

That way when you do start dating, their competition isn't other men, it is you!

And that is the best competition, because you'll know exactly how to be treated.

It's perfect! It is amazing!

Lovers Key

It's the best feeling in the world!

Love yourself more!

Lovers Key, my favorite place to be!

I love, love, love lovers key!

Lovers Key is a state park with miles of hiking trails and a beautiful beach. You get the best of both worlds! I go there often to go on nature walks, workouts, or to watch the sunset. I've been doing date night Saturday nights by myself. I'll walk/workout on the nature trails and then bring a cheese tray and wine and sit and watch the sunset. It's so nice. I really do enjoy my time alone now. Thinking and being.

However, every time I go there now, I'm reminded how Jill told me that Eric brought her to the Lovers Key Resort one weekend, which is right across the road, and I see it every time I'm there. It's very crushing to know that at one of your favorite places to go, you're reminded that he was there with another woman.

But still I go, I will not allow him to ruin everything in my life. I just hope someday, I won't think about him being with someone else every time I'm there. I've thought about getting myself a room there, just to try and make a new memory. I'm not sure if and how that will help or if it would be torture. But I'm trying to make new memories. Traveling to new places by myself on my year of healing and self-love and this may just be what I need!

I've gone to Asheville and Charleston all by myself this year. What great experiences those were…this would just further my healing journey and help me more.

My Stay at Lovers Key: A Self Love Saturday, June 20, 2020

I took myself out for a Saturday Nature Trail Hop. I went to four different nature trails.

First, I went to Six Mile Cypress Slough, next to the Koreshan State Historic Site and then to Freedom Park and ended up at Lovers Key.

Each one was great. Six Mile slough is my second favorite nature walk, after Lovers Key. Cypress slough is amazing. It's all boardwalk overlooking the water and the cypress trees and knees. It looks like something out of a fairy tale, especially in the summer. The morning is amazing with the light shining through the leaves, the brilliant color of the trees and the pretty blue color of the sky. It is the best. I met a gentleman there, we talked for a little bit. It's always nice meeting new people on the journey.

Next, I went to Koreshan State Park, this a historical location and campsite. This walk is short but beautiful. Many places to sit and take in all the beautiful spots that overlook the Estero River that have beautiful hanging trees with moss hanging down that make a beautiful spot to sit, think and admire nature. The nature trail leads you to the Koreshan Unity settlement with the historic buildings and these two historic bridges that I love to walk to and admire. Another favorite of mine. Next, I went to Freedom Park, another short but beautiful walk. That day I seen a cloud that looked like an angel. I love angels and I do believe in signs and I believe they were telling me that I was on the right track and to keep going.

Next, I went to check into my room at Lovers Key Resort. It was about 2:00, check-in was four, so I'm early like normal. My room wasn't ready yet, so I went down to the bar/restaurant to get a glass of champagne, and sat out by the water. It was beautiful and peaceful and I was so content and happy. I checked into the room after that. The room was beautiful! It was a suite, on a high level that overlooked the bay. It had a kitchen, living room area, a spacious bedroom, and the bathroom had a jacuzzi in it. The large lanai extended out from the bedroom to the living room. It was amazing. With a perfect view of the beach and back bay.

At first, I was overwhelmed with sadness and started to cry because I couldn't believe he'd take her somewhere so beautiful and then because I like to torture myself, I pictured him there with her. And I wondered if I was in the same room as them, sat at the same table as them, rode on the same elevator…

My first thought was "I'm going to get drunk. I need shots!" But I quickly pulled myself out of that moment and told myself, "I am here for me, for my self-healing. You wanted to do this, pull yourself together and have a nice time."

It's okay to throw yourself a pity party, just make sure to pull yourself out of it quickly. This is your life; don't let someone who never deserved you, ruin it. Give yourself the necessary time you need, cry, scream, get angry, mourn… but always, always put yourself back together…only this time you'll be so much stronger that no one will get you down again!

I brought myself a self-love care package of pink roses, some cheese, Norman Love chocolates, and a bottle of champagne…in a pretty pink sparkly bottle that I kept. I do treat myself well. Someone has to do it and it might as well be me!

I poured myself a glass of champagne (which was a mistake, I might add). And set out to go to my favorite nature trail at 4:00 p.m. In the middle of the Florida heat, drinking champagne. It was nice, but very, very hot! I thought I might die at one time. Champagne was not the ideal liquid to be drinking on a hot summer's day! I made it through the walk and headed back into my room. On the elevator up to my room, there was two ladies on with us and one was so funny. I thought to myself, *they seem like fun people*. I didn't think much of it and got off on my floor. Got to my room, showered, and put my dress on that I was wearing for my dinner date night with myself!

I went down to Flippers on the Bay, the Lovers Keys restaurant. It had an hour wait and I asked if I could just stand by the bar, and they said yes. I went to the bar and ordered myself another champagne and stood there by the bar and then ordered a crab cake. Eric actually turned me onto crab cakes. I never knew I liked them until he made some for me one day…now I'm hooked. Makes my heart hurt now just thinking about it. Anyway, the chef came out and brought me a stool so I could sit down. I kept telling them I was okay. I can stand; I don't mind, but they insisted. The people sitting beside me got their table and the next people to come sit by me were the two ladies from the elevator.

They were my age, funny, and having a good time. I said something to the lady beside me that she had said in the elevator, and we immediately hit it off and we were talking, laughing, and having a good time. They asked me why I was here alone and I told them a glimpse of the story and they were like, "Oh my God, you need something harder than champagne!" So, they bought me a round of drinks and ended up paying for my dinner. They were the sweetest and I was having such a good time.

After that I walked up to my room, a little buzzed at this point. I watched the sunset from my lanai, drank my champagne, ate my cheese and chocolates, and just sat, in silence, just sat, thinking.

Then it was time for my self-love jacuzzi bath! Then I went to bed.

The next morning, I woke up at 6:00 a.m., right when the sun was rising. It was so beautiful. I made myself coffee and sat out on the lanai, watched the sunrise, and read my book. It was amazing. It was such a great, healing trip and I was so happy I did this for myself.

Then I went to church to volunteer.

I love me more!

So much!

I am awesome.

I am amazing.

And I can do ANYTHING I put my mind to.

Someone will love me someday; I am certain of that.

I will be able to love someone again someday; I am certain of that.

But until then, I need to love myself the way I want to be loved, and then I will not settle for anything less than what I deserve. And I deserve the world.

Girlfriends

Surround yourself with uplifting understanding and supportive girlfriends. I am lucky enough to have the bestest friends in the world. Not one judged me for how long it took me to get over and move on and they all listened without condemning me. I'm sure some of them wanted to smack me at times, but they were all patient and kind. I am thankful for the tribe of girlfriends I have by my side. Without them I don't know if would have made it.

When the pandemic started, a friend of mine, Tami, and I started a book and wine club. At first it was twice a week and the then once a week. Plus, we started talking almost daily and joked around how we are going to start a club for single women. I cherish this friend and we have become so much closer, even though we live states away. She has become one of my best friends and one I can rely on the most. These times we spend together are very refreshing, fun and fulfilling. I also met some friends at my condo and we do a happy hour every Saturday evening. It's been a fun and liberating year of growth. From old friends to new friends and growing friendships. Friends I see every once in a while, and friends I talk to on the phone. I cherish each and every one and I am so thankful.

Thanksgiving with Christine, Irish Fest and Japanese with Audrey, book club with Tami and Tracie, massage, cheese, and wine days with Ann and dinner with Susan. Here's to all my best friends to new friends: Donna, Lily, Dana, Stephanie, and all my fellow church and volleyball friends and many, many more along the way. I'm thankful to be single and to be able to do everything and see everything I have done solo, but we are never meant to live life solo, pick up friendships along the way, and cherish them. I feel so blessed to have met so many people in the past year with all the adventures I've taken!

You're never really alone, when you have a tribe of girlfriends by your side. Girlfriends are so important whether you're single or with someone else. We cannot do life successfully and happy without GOOD girlfriends, friendships, and connections.

Girlfriends have been a huge part of my healing and growth, and I will be forever thankful and gracious to them all. I love each and every single one of them.

Healing Journey Continued
Part 2

Your new life is going to cost you your old one.
It's going to cost you your comfort zone and your sense of direction.
It's going to cost you relationships and friends.
It's going to cost you being liked and understood.
But it doesn't matter.
Because people who are meant for you are going to meet you on the other side.
And you're going to build a new comfort zone around
the things that actually move you forward.
And instead of being liked, you're going to be loved.
Instead of being understood, you're going to be seen.
All you're going to lose is what was built for a person you no longer are.
LET IT GO!

-Briana Wiest

September 2021

I have grown so much in the last year. I have grown in my life, emotionally, physically, mentally, and financially. I have much more growing to do and I'm definitely not where I want to be but every day, I'm getting there and I'm so, so much better than I was a year ago…two years ago. I can actually say, I love myself and I'm so proud of who I've become, and this is the first time in my whole life I can say that AND actually mean it! This is the first time in my life that I've felt true happiness and didn't feel ashamed and hated myself. I've come, not only to see my worth but acknowledge and demand my worth and not settling for anything less…in EVERY area of my life. ANY thing that does not bring me absolute JOY, I just don't do it. ANY one who does not add value to my life with joy, respect, and peace, they are no longer are a part of my life; I've cut them out. THIS is MY life, and I WILL live it the way I choose to. Happy, abundant, loved… This next year, is a life-changer and I'm so glad I took that year of self-love and healing journey because now I'm living my best life. Sure I have a long way to go…I'm just getting started and I have so much further to go!

The second part of my healing journey starts after I finally found out about the third girl in April 2019. The beginning of COVID. The first part of the healing journey, I kept going back and forth and talking with him, and you can't truly heal when you can't let it go. This is where my true healing began. With no contact at all. I did not speak to him for over a year now. I finally let him go and I finally became so much stronger and I can finally say that I'm so proud of myself. And I know I will keep getting stronger. So much has happened in this last year and a half, my life is beyond amazing, and it will just keep getting better!

When COVID hit, I freaked out like the rest of us. Being a small-business owner with a massage therapy practice. I couldn't work (or wasn't supposed to). The two weeks we were shut down, I stayed in and that's when my drinking started. From morning to evening. Morning mimosas or Bloody Marys to wine in the evening. Cleaned and gardened. Tried to stay sane.

After the two weeks, I was still scared to work, and I still could not go into work. But one by one clients would reach out to me for in-home massages. And I told myself; well, if I'm going to work and put my life on the line, I'm working for full price (I use to do discounted packages). Before I went anywhere, I asked if they were healthy or had traveled, and if everything seemed okay, I'd go over there. First it started with one client, twice a week, and then one by one, people would reach out to me…soon, I was doing really good, and making good money in the middle of a pandemic. I thought to myself, "THIS is how I want my life to be like!" In the middle of COVID, my life changed.

I decided I'm raising ALL of my prices. I refuse to make less than $100 per massage. I've been doing massage for twenty years, and I'm damn good at it and I have the many reviews to prove it. I specialize in therapeutic/medical massage. For years, I never felt right charging what I wanted and felt bad and for some reason I never felt like I deserved it or was worth it, even though I knew I was, but deep down, I never did feel worthy.… But NOW I know I'm worthy of every penny, and my clients pay me above and beyond my asking price. Once I realized my worth, I won't settle for anything less, that's when my life changed. I've worked so hard to be where I am right now, and it's just the beginning. I'm so excited to see where my life will go now, now that I've come to KNOW my worth!

Worth…such a powerful and IMORTANT word.

Make sure you know your worth and never settle for less. Your life will change…YOU will change!

This past year of healing really changed me…when you put yourself first for once…everything changes. I'm a brand-new person and I love me more! Not only do I love me more…I FINALLY actually LOVE myself. I still have my healing process and I'm still on my journey, but I'm a lot further than I use to be!

When, deep down, you've hated yourself for years, you accept and tolerate abusive, bad, and unfair behavior. You accept less than you deserve. Change that thinking.

It takes time to change deep-seated trauma. You have to be gentle with yourself and show up for yourself. You are worth it.

You deserve more.

You deserve the world.

I started taking Life Coaching classes to become a life coach in June. It was a six-month, online virtual class. Another great healing process for me. I am now an Internationally Certified Life Coach through Symbiosis!

I started a business called Empowered Women Life Coaching. My goal is to help codependent woman find strength and true happiness. I also help women reach their goals, whatever they may be.

If I can go from codependent to independent, and it be the best healing process I've ever done and now living my best life…I want to help other women live their best lives and break those chains! We all are little codependent; it's when its extreme and unhealthy that it is detrimental.

I also started a blog called Wander Woman: finding courage, confidence, and strength within the journey of a million miles. I blog about traveling solo, with friends, or family. Budget friendly or extravagant stays.

Since this all happened, I've traveled alone four times. And several times with friends. I want to see as many places as I can possibly see. You can say I've become addicted to traveling and want to travel every couple of months! I want to be a beacon of light for others. To prove it can be done, to help others come out of their cave and come into the light. Plus, the happiness and freedom, I find with traveling, especially alone. There is so much strength in that. When you can go anywhere alone and be happy, you can do anything!

I've went to Asheville for my first solo trip, and Charleston for Valentine's Day alone, and then I went to Sedona in April 2021 to see the red rocks and visit the vortexes and work on this book.

I recently went on a ninety-day no alcohol diet and a ten-day no sugar/carbs. I wanted to see how my body did without it. Currently I'm on day forty-five of ninety no alcohol. I got to a point that I drank way too much and every day. The last time I drank, I drank a whole bottle of wine and then opened another bottle. I decided I needed to take a break and do ninety days sober to see if I have a problem and see how I feel. I feel much better, more focused, more present, no more headaches or fogginess. I just feel much better all around. Mood, energy, physically, and mentally! I've been a better mother, for sure. Better massage therapist, getting way more things done, and doing better with EVERYTHING I do!

Even when I do start back up, I definitely won't drink like I did and only once in a while and not much, I definitely don't want to feel the way it makes me feel in the mornings or in general.

Here is what happened in the past year…this year was more about building friendships and adding adventures with friends…but still taking care of me and doing solo trips, because this has become important to me. And from now on, I do what I want. I'm not hurting anyone and when that certain someone comes into my life, he will be supportive of me and love me for who I am.

I had dated someone for four months, two months ago. And it started out great, like it usually does, but little by little, he became controlling and very jealous, and tried to get me to stop playing volleyball. He was amazing in so many ways, but he had/has deep-seated insecurities that I couldn't help or tolerate any longer, and after several fights, I thought, in the beginning, he just needed time and we just needed time. But I grew to realize that he wasn't ever going to change and he wanted me to change and wanted to control me and be a codependent woman, that I no longer am anymore. I feel like life gave me a test and I passed. I got out of this relationship before it had too much hold on me. The thing about any relationship… is it's okay to want what you want and not want something. That's okay, just let go and move on.

When you realize it's not going to work, it's of no fault of either person. There is someone who will love what you love and want what you want. Don't settle and let it be. Just let it be. Let love come to you in whatever form it comes. Maybe it's just in friendships, your passion, your work. Don't go out frantically looking for or even wishing or wanting. Learn to love yourself and be your own "Love" first and the rest will follow. I'm to the point now, that I don't want, nor need someone in my life to complete me and this is the first time in my whole forty-two years that I can honestly say I'm happy alone. Would I want someone. Yes, eventually, if it's good for me and "us" as a relationship. But I can go without it and I am happy, my boys are happy and THAT is all that matters.

For the longest time I searched and never thought I'd be complete until I was with someone and found someone for my boys and THEN I'd be happy and have the family I always wanted, always thought I'd have. The happy family all young girls grow up believing your life should be like. This version of life many of us have stuck in our minds of how life "should" be can truly mess EVERYTHING up. So, for years I've been in search of love, that I settled for crap! Crap! ALL THE TIME! I'm so embarrassed by some of the things I did and tolerated, just because I never thought I was truly good enough, so I accepted anything just to "feel" some sort of love, I felt so alone…to be in search of this so-called life were supposed to be living! That's all crap! This whole time, I've had these amazing boys who looked up to me and would have been fine with just me, but I searched and searched for a love that never existed for me, for this "family" I already had with my boys. I had to find that love inside of me. Now I can be the mom I need to be for my amazing young men.

The one thing that stuck in my head, after the breakup with Eric is my youngest boy said to me, "Mom, I don't think you should date anymore. I don't want to see you cry anymore." And for the first time since I left their father, I KNOW "just the three of us" is JUST fine! Now I spend my time and focus on them.

Summer Road Trip to Georgia, June 2020

For summer this year, since COVID went rampant, the boys and I went to Georgia to visit my best friend, Tami. We go visit her every year on our summer road trips up north. We normally go all the way up to Iowa, but with COVID, we only went up to see Tami and came back. It's always nice seeing her and hanging out. We hung out by the river, the boys and I went to see an animal sanctuary one day for the boys and on our way back, we went to go see Providence Canyon (the mini–Grand Canyon). It was pretty neat. We had a nice time, always a nice time at Tami's. It was different this time as she herself was going through a bad breakup and since then we have gotten really close.

Tami's 50th Birthday Adventure, Savannah, November 2020

What a trip. Tracie and I flew up to Atlanta and Tami picked us up and then we drove to Savannah for a weekend we will never forget. We stayed at the Marshall House, right in the historic district, which was walking distance to everything. The hotel was amazing, we had a suite, but only one bathroom between three ladies. Fun times. We got there on a Thursday and stayed three nights. We had a great time walking around city, sightseeing, taking funny pictures, partying, and drinking way too much! Friday morning was really rough for me, as I drank way more than I should have. I wasn't "well" until twelve when I made myself eat something. We would start early, with morning mimosas or Bloody Marys. The girls wanted to get the Bloody Marys with the oysters in them…me? I like them regular. It really was a fun time walking around through all the shops and bar. Every night we ended up at the same dance club. It was the best place there to dance. Good times.

What happens in Savannah stays in Savannah. It was a great experience traveling and spending time with friends. It's always fun to be with friends, but when I'm with friends, it is quite a bit of a different experience than when I'm alone. I like my time with friends, more about drinking, hanging out, laughing, and having fun. When I'm alone, I'm doing more inner work, exploring, and enjoying…and not really doing much at all. I like both, but I really like my solo trips.

Charleston, Valentine's Day 2021

The past two years now, I've went to Charleston for Valentine's Day, this time my best friend Tami joined me. We had a great time together, exploring the city together. We went to a lot of the same places as I went to the year before. We had great dinners and drinks, went dancing, wine tasting, breweries, and more. Next year we said we were going to bring our significant other with us, but as of now, I'm not sure either of us will have one and it may just be us again! Which I'm totally fine with. I've decided I'd much rather be alone than treated less than I desire and deserve. I'm happy alone now and that is huge.

Sedona, April 2021

Sedona was AMAZING! I stayed at the most beautiful and amazing bed and breakfast called Canyon Villa. It was beautiful. I stayed in a room that overlooked the Bell Rock. All the rocks where amazing! Such a beautiful place! The time change was a lot for me to get used to. It is a three-hour difference.

So, I barely made it to sunset every night, however, I got up every morning between four and five and went out to the main area and set up a spot that overlooked the Bell Rock to work on this book. I would work on it and then go walk the trails at sunrise and go exploring. I made it to several rocks including Cathedral Rock, Devil's Bridge, Bell Rock, and many more.

It was really neat meeting everyone that were staying there. I met a lot of them while working on my book and we'd talk about what everyone was doing and what everyone has seen. I even met a really nice couple that I saw in the Grand Canyon too! I mean what are the odds! I'm so honored and happy to meet so many nice people on my journeys! The people who worked at the bed and breakfast were really kind too and asked me about my book and wanted to be able to display it in their store. I felt so honored and loved. It is a great place and I will be staying there again when I go back!

One day I booked a Vortex Jeep tour. That was amazing. We went to several rocks and we learned that the energy goes in a spiral so the trees would grow in a spiral. It was interesting. We went to a Buddhist Temple called Amitabha Stupa and Peace Park; it was amazing. It had these prayer wheels that you'd turn and say your prayers and it would send out healing energy. A meditation platform and the 36-foot enlightenment Stupa; the Buddha of limitless light, you would walk around the Stupa clockwise three or more times for healing. It was an amazing experience. And then we went to the Rachel's Knoll another Vortex with a lot of healing energy. It was a nice tour.

Then I went and walked around downtown Sedona for a little while, checking out all the shops.

My favorite I'd have to say was walking Bell and the Courthouse Rocks. So incredibly breathtaking. I loved every minute of it. My only regret is being in such a hurry through all of them that I only got to walk half of every one of them. Next time I will be taking my time and only picking out a couple and making sure I get through all of it. I will definitely be doing Bell and Courthouse over again and the Devil's Bridge.

Sunday, I took myself on a winery tour and went to a couple in Sedona: Page Springs and Javalina Vineyards. Those two were my favorites…actual vineyards. I went to the Page Springs the night before to have dinner and a bottle of wine. It was very good. Then the next day I started at Javalina and then headed to a nearby city called Cottonwood. It was a cute little town full of shops and restaurants. They had eight wineries! Eight! So, I picked four to go to. Each place I went to I had a tasting and an appetizer of some sort. After that I went to the Airport Mesa Vortex. It was interesting walking that trail a little buzzed. I tried so hard to make it to sunset, but I just couldn't and went back to my room. The next day, my last day in Sedona, I got up, worked on my book, and went to Devil's Bridge to walk that trail before I headed to the Grand Canyon.

The drive to the Grand Canyon alone, was beautiful…yet sometimes scary but the scenery was breathtaking, driving through Coconino National Forest…another place I want to see when I visit again. It looked so beautiful, I just wish I had more time to visit all the places I wanted to see. I was there five days and still not enough time!

I got to the Grand Canyon, right in time for my lunch reservations at one of their restaurants. I sat at a place that overlooked the canyon. I met and talked with a nice couple that was sitting near me. After I ate, I went for a little walk to see the Canyon and found myself walking the Bright Angel Trail that went down the canyon. It was amazing, but I was NOT prepared. I should have dropped all my stuff off and got several more waters. I walked quite a bit down, talking with some people I met on the way and enjoying this beautiful, wonderous view. It was amazing! I was halfway down and decided I should go head back up. The down part was the easy part…the way up was brutal! Thank goodness, I do the stair climber a lot in the gym! Boy, I didn't know if I'd make it! But I did and it was a great experience. I checked into my room at the Maswik Lodge that is located inside the park. It was such a nice place, on the bottom floor that walked out to the back where you could have a bonfire or cookout. I loved this room and hotel. I just stayed in for the evening and took a bath, relaxed, and journaled and was in bed early so the next morning, I could watch the sunrise over the Canyon.

I book all or most of my stays through Hotels.com, which I love because after ten stays, I get one free night stay somewhere and I've stayed at some pretty cool places. However, if you book through Airbnb, you get to pick out some different, unique stays for cheap. It all depends on what type of vacation you want. The main purpose is to get out and see the beautiful and amazing.

The next morning, I got up early, checked out of the hotel and went to walk around the canyon. It literally was breathtaking. So peaceful, so calm. You just felt like nothing else mattered. As I walked and every time I turned to look into the canyon, every time…every. Single. Time, it took my breath away. I had people take many pictures of me doing cool yoga poses as they walked by. At one of the overlooks, I ran into the couple from the Sedona bed and breakfast and we had a good conversation. I'm sure everyone wanted to know why I was traveling alone, and I love to show people that it is okay to travel alone. It builds strength, confidence, and a since of pride.

From there, I headed back on a four-hour drive into Phoenix, where I was staying for the night, before I got on the early flight back home.

What a spectacular, beautiful, wonderous, healing and fulfilling trip! I LOVED every minute of it!

Summer Road Trip to Iowa, June/July 2021

This year the boys and I had a great trip up to Iowa. First, we went camping at Ginnie Springs in Northern Florida for two days and went tubing down the river. It was a really cool place. Kind of loud at night and wish we would have stayed in a different location there. Lots of pretty places that overlooked the river that we could have put the tent. If we do more camping, I definitely need to build up my camping supplies! I brought a huge cooler full of food. We cooked out every day. We had hamburgers; I made hobo dinners, where you take a hamburger patty, top with seasoned salt and pepper and then top with onions and sliced potatoes, wrap in aluminum foil and you can put them in a bonfire or on top of the grill. They are the best. The Springs are just beautiful. It rained a couple of times, so we stayed in the tent and played cards until it stopped.

From there we headed up to Alabama to see Tami, and stayed with her a couple of days. She brought us to a waterfall area one day and we just explored and swam. The boys love doing stuff like that. At Tami's house, she has a bunch of trails out back and a golf cart, so the boys went out on that and had a great time. The boys love seeing Tami.

Next, we went to Gatlinburg, Tennessee. What a cool little area! Loved it up here, in the mountains. We stayed in a cabin in the mountains. It was so cool. It had a spa outside and a heart-shaped jacuzzi inside. It was hilarious when both the boys put their swim trunks on to sit in the heart-shaped tub. You know I got a picture of that and will be framing that later! Ha! We cooked-out there. We had grilled chicken one day and hobo dinners the next. The next morning we went into Gatlinburg. We walked around a bit to find some breakfast and then we went to the Anakeesta Park where you ride up on a sky lift to the top of the mountain and it has a treetop skywalk. We rode the mountain coaster, which Michael lost his phone on it. Yeah, he'll never forget that! Andrew did some gem mining and we walked around and had lunch in one of the restaurants. It was pretty cool. I just wish I got tickets for the ziplines. The boys would have wanted to do that. Maybe our next adventure we will do some ziplining! It's definitely worth it.

That night we went back to the cabin. We started a bonfire out front. The boys were playing in the creek out front, catching salamanders. I was sitting by the fire. I heard some commotion coming across the road in the trees, and all of a sudden, the boys yell, BEAR! I jump up, say a choice word that rhymes with TRUCK! I look over and notice he's all the way across the road, and the porch is very close to us, so I yell, RUN! All of us ran to the porch, and as we get there, the adolescent bear runs by us up the mountain. I managed to snap a picture of him. The poor bear just looked scared and we were not under any threat. You really shouldn't run from bears, but we were far enough away from him and he wasn't after us anyway. That was something to see.

The next day we headed up to Southern Illinois. We went there two years ago and it was something beautiful and I never got to see everything I wanted to see. On our way into Illinois, the GPS, brought us on a way, I had to use a ferry to get over the river. As I'm sitting there, it didn't quite dawn on me "a ferry" at that point I was getting tired and just wanted to get there. I was irritated but really what a cool experience! First car ferry, we had ever been on.

And then we got lost trying to get to the place we were staying. That was the worst of our trip. I guess what do you expect on road trips? One thing I will be working on, is NOT losing my patience and cool on the road trips. It's bound to happen when you're driving in unknown places. Just stop and take a breath. Everything will be just fine. Breathe! But we made it. We were staying at the same place we stayed at two years ago, and had a good couple days there. We went to Burden Falls and Rim Rock, which someone told us to go see, which was my favorite. It was so beautiful.

From there we headed to Iowa and stayed with my family. I'm usually there through the 4th. It's always really nice to see my family and spend time with all of them! I went to Cedar Ridge with Liz, the water park with Becca and Mellany, Amana's with Mom, and dinners most every night with the whole family. It was a nice time seeing all of them.

From there we drove all the way to New Orleans and stayed there a couple of days and walked around the city and then headed back home! What a great, successful summer road trip!

Alabama, October 2021

End of my healing journey for my book and beginning of the next stage of my life!

I have been really wanting to see fall this year, so I'm going to see my best friend and the fall colors! I'm so excited. We are going to go see Lookout Mountain in Alabama. It looks beautiful! I can't wait.

My future travel plans...

I would like to head up to Asheville mid to late October this year and in early December, I'm planning another solo trip to Chicago! My first city solo trip. And I will be focusing on safety first. But I am *sooooo* excited to go to Chicago. I'm just really hoping that COVID won't get out of hand and the city won't shut down. So, I'll see about all that. And Utah in April.

I'm already planning our next summer family trip for 2022. This time, there will be a surprise on the way up. We are doing an East Coast trip and going to see my aunt Linda in Ohio, where my mom will be flying in for Aunt Linda's birthday, and from there, we will be going to northern Michigan, by the water, Pictured Rocks National Lakeshore and much, much more! Surprises to come!

Then, next October, Salem Massachusetts! Amongst many more!

Be sure to check out my travel blog at www.thewanderwoman.blog to follow and keep up with all the fun and amazing trips I'm taking!

My goal is to be traveling every couple of months, journaling and blogging about every trip. From solo, family, and friends! And…some day as a couple!

Keep your individuality.
Keep loving what makes you, YOU!
Keep your spark.
Then others will be drawn to you,
So you can help them find theirs!
Do what makes you happy.
Your people will find you.
Don't let anyone take
Your spark,
Keep shinning.